TALKING WITH ADVENTURERS

CONVERSATIONS WITH
Christina M. Allen • Robert Ballard • Michael L. Blakey
Ann Bowles • David Doubilet
Jane Goodall • Dereck & Beverly Joubert
Michael Novacek • Johan Reinhard • Rick C. West
and Juris Zarins

COMPILED AND EDITED BY
Pat Cummings and Linda Cummings, Ph.D.

NATIONAL GEOGRAPHIC SOCIETY

Washington, D.C.

Published by the
National Geographic Society
1145 17th Street N.W.
Washington, D.C. 20036

John M. Fahey, Jr.
President and Chief Executive Officer

Gilbert M. Grosvenor
Chairman of the Board

Nina D. Hoffman
Senior Vice President

William R. Gray
Vice President & Director of the Book Division

The maps by Carl Mehler, National Geogaphic Society Director of Maps, Book Division, Joe Ochlak, Map Researcher, and Jehan Aziz, Map Production, do not show all of the places where the adventurers have worked. They were created to indicate where expedition sites talked about in this book are found.

Library of Congress Cataloging-in-Publication Data
Talking With Adventurers:
conversations with Christina M. Allen, Robert Ballard, Michael L. Blakey, Ann Bowles, David Doubilet, Jane Goodall, Dereck & Beverly Joubert, Michael Novacek, Johan Reinhard, Rick C. West, and Juris Zarins /compiled and edited by Pat Cummings and Linda Cummings, Ph.D.
p.   cm.
Includes bibliographical references.
Summary: Twelve men and women who work in the field of science discuss and explain their occupations, including what they might do in a normal working day and the scariest thing that ever happened to them.
ISBN 0-7922-7068-1
1. Scientists—Interviews—Juvenile literature. 2. Scientists—biography—Juvenile literature. [1. Scientists. 2. Occupations.] I. Allen, Christina M. II. Cummings, Pat. III. Cummings, Linda C., 1948–
Q141.T33   1998
509.2'2—dc21
[B]   98-11457

Printed in the United States of America

10 9 8 7 6 5 4 3 2 1

For Chuku
— *Pat*

For Kalila and Keija
— *Linda*

CONTENTS

Dear Reader,

Can you imagine yourself face-to-face with a man-eating shark or sitting all alone under the stars on a hilltop in an African forest? If you've ever been the one in your class who raised a hand to ask why or how or what if, you might have a lot in common with the adventurers in this book.

Some of the people you'll meet here asked questions as kids that they are still answering today. Maybe the ocean seemed mysterious, or they sensed there were secrets hidden in deserts or high up on mountaintops. Maybe they asked questions about animals and insects and even human behavior that no one could answer for them. Curiosity got these adventurers started; finding an answer often led them to ask other questions. Whether their questions had to do with dinosaurs or ancient people or how animals communicate, some of the answers you'll find in the library today might be based on their discoveries.

Teachers and parents can point you to books and experiments that might answer questions you have. But imagine hearing about a long-lost sunken ocean liner and then actually going to hunt for it. Imagine the dusty tip of your shoe bumping against a dinosaur bone bleached white by time and the sands of a desert. Imagine a tarantula crawling slowly up your arm, and your only thought being to carefully study its movements. Imagination moved all of the adventurers in this book from curiosity to exploration.

Each person in the book tells about how he or she got interested in the subject that became a life's work. Each answers the same ten questions that we put together with the help of some thoughtful and inquisitive young students. Unfamiliar words are listed in the Glossary. Each adventurer has some advice to share. Some of them have special projects that you can check out right away if their work appeals to you.

As you get to know the 12 people in this book, you might be surprised to find that, different as they are, they have a lot in common. Some had parents and teachers and friends who encouraged them; all have stories about obstacles they've faced, physical hardships they endure, and the incredible amount of writing and reading and research that backs up their discoveries. They all love their work with a passion that makes the danger and loneliness and patient documentation just part of their job. So when you open an encyclopedia or pop in a video or press your nose to the glass in a museum to see what they've found, you'll know how it all started. Here are the adventurers' own stories, their own answers to the whys, the hows, and the what ifs that they once asked.

Linda Cummings

Pat Cummings

Christina M. Allen

RAIN FOREST ECOLOGIST
Birthday: April 8, 1970

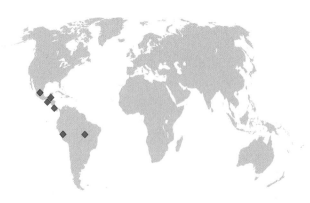

You might say I began my career when I was a baby. When I was two, my mom found me in the yard pouring an entire jar of worms all over my lap to study them. From then on, my parents nurtured my love of other creatures, encouraged my interests, and respected me for having the ability to observe nature's tiny details. It was my job to alert the family to the presence of a beautiful bird, a bug, or a bright red mushroom. They even let me bring stray animals home to care for and nurse back to health.

When I was six, my parents packed me, my sister, and our dog into a van and drove from Washington, D.C., to Alaska. My first year of school in Anchorage was hard. I tried four grade schools, spending more time in the principal's office than in class, before we finally found a new school that fit my personality and learning style. Along with traditional books and exercises, we used computers, conducted science experiments, studied an ant colony, and went on field trips.

My dad was a lawyer, but in his spare time he was also a pilot. He taught me self-reliance in the wilderness and an even deeper appreciation for animals. Once, while flying together, I spotted a lone wolf on a mountain far below, so we landed and tracked it on foot. The wolf let us get within 20 feet. Then we just stared at each other. I thought I'd be scared, but the wolf's furry coat and brown eyes were so beautiful that my fear evaporated.

My dad and I would fly to a remote Alaskan river where grizzly bears came together to eat salmon. It can be dangerous to be in close proximity to bears, especially if you find yourself between a mother bear and her cub. So before we arrived, my dad decided that I should learn to shoot a rifle, just in case. Landing on a sandbank, we set up some cans for me to try to shoot. I was doing so well that we didn't notice the tide rising. When we turned toward the plane and saw it surrounded with water, we screamed, realizing that we could be stranded in the wilderness with the plane 20 feet underwater. We acted, and fast! Jumping in the plane, we started the engine, but the wheels tugged in the mud. It felt like forever, but eventually we pulled free. We skimmed through the fast-rising tide to finally lift off with whoops of relief. I realized that part of the thrill of doing something scary is how you feel afterward. Knowing that you reacted the right way gives you confidence and makes you feel capable of conquering other tough things.

My father's death in a plane crash while I was in college had an unexpected effect on me. Instead of making me retreat to a safer lifestyle, the event solidified his teachings. He always lived life to the fullest, and I realized that life is too short to let anything get in the way of what you want. I had always wanted to see the rain forest, so I went off to study ecology in the rain forests of Brazil. After that, I knew I wanted to go to graduate school to become a rain forest ecologist.

In graduate school, I went to the Peruvian Amazon to study tapirs, deer, and peccaries with a great Amazon researcher, Dr. Richard Bodmer. Later, anthropologist Dr. Allan Burns told me about MayaQuest, an interactive program that lets kids in classrooms direct a live expedition in Central America via the Internet. The team needed a rain forest ecologist; it sounded perfect for me. After four months of persistence, I got the job.

Five other team members and I spent six weeks in the jungle exploring mysteries of the ancient Maya. The experience combined my interests in ecology, conservation, and exploration. For the future we plan quests on every continent. This adventure could last a lifetime!

What was the job that got you started in your field?

I started not with a job but with my decision to go to the Brazilian rain forest to study ecology, and to study it further when I got back. There may not be a job that is exactly what you want; maybe the job doesn't exist yet. But follow your passion. Even if you take a job just to make money, there are 16 hours a day that only you will decide how to spend. Some famous researchers and inventors made their discoveries during their time off.

What was the scariest thing that ever happened in your work?

We were in Costa Rica, a day's ride from help. It was dark, and I was checking nets we had set up to find out what bat species lived in the area. When I felt a prick on my shoulder, I shone my headlamp around but saw nothing. The thought that it might have been a snakebite nagged at me, and an hour later I felt dizzy and nauseous.

The next day I found a snake at the same spot where I had been the night before. My instructor, a snake expert, took a look at my shoulder and identified a pit viper bite and the snake as being from the highly poisonous *lateralis* species. Apparently it had not injected venom, or I might have died. In coming close to losing my life, I felt lucky to be alive and to be able to have so many unusual, exciting, and adventurous experiences. But I also vowed to be more careful.

Eye swollen from a wasp sting, Allen examines an Amazonian snail.

"Random opportunities can shape your life. Expose yourself to many different activities...a sport, an academic subject, a craft. Learn as much as you can about what interests you, not being afraid to drop it if something more fascinating comes along. There are too many joys in life to limit yourself."

Christina Allen

Allen sits on a platform in the Peruvian Amazon. Nights waiting for animals to visit piles of fruit she had left for them were, she says, "Scary!"

How do you choose a project?

For a scientist, choosing a project and a question to answer is the most difficult, yet most important, thing. Lots of money and time can be spent trying to answer a trivial question. I mostly look for what is unknown in the areas of study that I'm interested in. If you are doing what fascinates you, you may uncover important information even if you don't exactly answer the question you posed. Creativity, intuition, and opportunity are as important in science as they are in any pursuit.

I worked out a new method in wildlife ecology only because I didn't listen to people who criticized me for being unconventional and a risk taker. I also tend to pick my projects based on the animals. I especially like animals that are misunderstood. For example, bats are thought to be evil and dirty, but they are very important to the ecosystem. I also like to study animals that are linked to traditional cultures. Without certain animals to hunt, many Amazonian cultures would die. Given a particularly great opportunity to make a discovery, I may be willing to risk more dangers. I am drawn to challenging situations.

All part of the job: Allen interviews archaeologist Dr. Peter Dunham at the Bladen Forest Reserve, in Belize.

Where do you work?

I've worked in Central and South America—Costa Rica, Guatemala, Belize, Brazil, Peru—and in Mexico. I go to sites in a variety of ways: by jeep, canoe, and even by ferryboat in the Amazon rain forest. For MayaQuest, we arrived at study sites by bicycle, by far the most fun way I've traveled yet! I used to think that I wouldn't go to the rain forests of Malaysia because leeches there drop from trees and suck your blood. But I'd go if the project were interesting enough.

What is a normal working day like for you?

In the field, my working day is never really "normal"—it varies from day to day. Usually, my activities involve walking in the forest checking for tracks and other animal signs. I look at plants and fruits for evidence of their being eaten by certain animals, interview local people about their hunting practices and knowledge of the environment, and write down my observations and experiences.

Do you have any children? Is your family involved in your work?

No, I don't have any children, but I have two dogs who are like my kids—one of them I found in the Peruvian rain forest! He was so sick I thought he would die, so I vaccinated him, nursed him back to health, and brought him home on the plane. The dogs do everything possible with me. I'm even working on a trailer for them that I can pull behind my bike. The hardest thing about traveling is leaving my dogs behind, but my family is very supportive of my work and helps me take care of them. My mom and my sister have traveled to visit me at many of my research sites. They even climbed the Inca Trail with me in Peru.

What special preparations do you have to make for your work?

Since my close encounter with a snakebite, I always carry a snake venom extractor kit and antivenin, which gives me a sense of security as much as anything else. About a month before going anywhere, I'll have about 20 different checklists in operation, which I add to and subtract from in my spare time. It's so important to be prepared, especially going to the Amazon. Also, getting ready adds to my excitement about the trip.

What is the hardest part of your work?

Working project to project as a freelance scientist is not as secure as working for a company that provides a steady paycheck. It can be an adventure in itself just getting funding for a project, but the advantage is that I get to do exactly what I want while learning important skills, like proposal writing and salesmanship.

A long walk through the jungle leads to an ancient Maya cave in Belize.

Biking in Todo Santos, Guatemala, with MayaQuest team member Doug Mason

What was your biggest discovery? What are you most proud of?

The fruit from palm trees is the main food for many rain forest animals. When I was doing research in Peru for my master's degree, I wanted to learn how certain animals were being affected by people cutting down the trees. I drew smooth mud circles on the forest floor to determine how many fruits each type of animal had eaten by studying the tracks they left in the mud.

In science, we mostly hear about the big, glamorous discoveries, but often progress is made by the collective effort of many people doing very specific in-depth work and contributing to the body of knowledge in smaller ways. Six months after I finished my research, I met a biology student in Belize who had heard of my mud circles method and was using it in his own research! So my biggest discovery is perhaps less of a discovery and more a method that will help others make discoveries of their own.

What is left for you to explore?

The more I see and learn, the more I realize how much there is to see and learn. I don't think I'll ever feel like I've seen or done it all, which is a very exciting prospect. To me, the greatest challenge in the fields of ecology and conservation is for scientists and governments to work with local people to create protected areas. If people all over the world cooperate, we can make sure that the wide variety of animals and plants living today will still exist in the future.

Check it out:

MayaQuest

For the first time in 1995, a team of five explorers, led by Dan Buettner, bicycled to ruins in Mexico and Central America, met with on-site archaeologists, and tried to unlock the mystery behind the collapse of ancient Maya civilization. But the team wasn't alone. More than one million people—kids, teachers, and others—from around the globe helped to lead the expedition via the Internet.

Armed with high-tech equipment, the team linked to classrooms and computers around the world, letting followers lead the expedition, interact with archaeologists and experts, view images from the trip, and learn about the ancient Maya and contemporary Central America.

MayaQuest's talented team of archaeologists, rain forest experts, anthropologists, and epigraphers continues to search for clues that might reveal why the ancient Maya civilization disappeared more than 1,000 years ago. As team members explore tombs, navigate jungle rivers, interact with archaeologists, and meet modern Maya, you are invited to come along and develop your own theories. Join the team on similar expeditions in Africa, the Galápagos Islands, Australia, and China.

Find out more:

www.classroom.com
MayaQuest
2221 Rosecrans Blvd., Suite 221
El Segundo, CA 90245

Robert Ballard

EXPLORER
Birthday: June 30, 1942

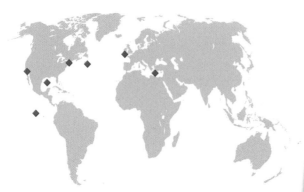

My love affair with the sea began when I was no more than six years old, walking along the sandy beaches of Southern California. I always wanted to make the first set of footprints in the wet sand.

My adventures began in small tidal pools carved in the rocks where creatures of all colors and shapes hid from view or darted back and forth, eager for the rising tide to set them free. Later my adventures took me out on a long pier near my home, where I spent countless hours dangling a baited hook beneath the sea, wondering what monster I might catch.

Unlike many surfers who sought the perfect wave, my interests always lay beneath the sea's surface in a world I could only imagine and dream of. Soon, wearing a snorkel and a mask, I made my first solo adventures in the deep. Later I would learn how to scuba dive, expanding my world of exploration many times over. All along the way, my parents and teachers encouraged my interest in the sea, providing me with books to read or taking me to the ocean once we moved inland and I couldn't reach it by myself.

Perhaps the greatest turning point in my life came when I was in high school and I wrote a letter to the famous Scripps Oceanographic Institution, in San Diego, asking how I might learn more about the sea.

A kind scientist answered my letter and told me how to apply to Scripps for a summer scholarship, which I received. During one of their cruises that summer, I met Dr. Robert Norris, a marine geologist. He loved the sea almost as much as I did. His passion was infectious. Soon he was asking me what my plans were and where I expected to attend college. I told him I didn't know, so he suggested I consider his school, the University of California in Santa Barbara.

My parents drove me to Santa Barbara for an interview, and one year later I drove there myself, this time as a member of the freshman class.

Now my love affair with the sea became a serious endeavor. If I wanted to be an undersea explorer, I needed to learn as much as I could about the laws of the physical world that controlled the environment I wanted to enter. The undersea world is not our natural world. It is unforgiving to those who make mistakes. At its greatest depths the water temperature is near freezing, the pressure is eight tons per square inch, and it is totally dark. It is easy to get lost in such a world. I needed to learn a lot about geography, navigation, meteorology, geology, biology, and many other things. While I was in school, I took a little of everything.

I decided another important thing for me to do was to join the U.S. Navy. If I was going to be an undersea explorer, I would have to lead men and women

on dangerous adventures where they might get hurt, and I didn't want that to happen. In the Navy I learned discipline, organization, and how to motivate and lead people on expeditions so that we could explore the wonders of the deep.

Finally, the time came to put all that I had learned to use, to go forth with a team of men and women and explore— an adventure I am still on and hope to be on for many years to come.

"Dream great dreams and then pursue them. And remember never to get into the thick of thin things. Study hard!"

Robert Ballard

Ballard in the hatch of the *Delta* sub in the Celtic Sea

What was the job that got you started in your field?

For three months, during the summer between my junior and senior years of high school, I went on one adventure after another while working at Scripps. On my first two times at sea, my ship was tossed about in an angry ocean. It was like a ride on a watery roller coaster. I was so impressed with the power of the sea and its ability to control my life.

What was the scariest thing that ever happened in your work?

I have had many scary moments—a fire in my submersible at 9,000 feet, or crashing into the side of a volcano at 20,000 feet. But perhaps the scariest experiences are when someone on my team is in danger: trapped in an undersea fissure or entangled in cables on a wreck. My profession can be dangerous. One must never take needless risks. Never tempt Neptune, the god of the sea, too far.

How do you choose a project?

I ask myself, is the project challenging? Has it ever been done before? Is it truly worth doing? Does it have importance to the world? I follow my own ideas and work on projects that I'm passionately interested in. Reading and research generate ideas for me.

Each project requires a great deal of long-term planning, so I have a number of projects all in various stages. Every project follows a five-year cycle: We first research the project to see if it's doable; then I look for a sponsor to provide the financial resources;

Named for scientist Allyn Vine, an early supporter of manned underwater research, the research submersible *Alvin* can carry a crew of three and can dive to 13,124 feet.

The *Alvin* submersible parks in the garage of its mother ship, *Lulu*.

then the project has to be organized; and finally, we get to go on the expedition. When the project is completed, there are articles to write for scientific journals or magazines, or perhaps a book or TV special to put together.

Where do you work?

When I'm not at sea, I work at the Institute for Exploration in Mystic, Connecticut, where we are building a research center and public exhibition center, including a deepwater aquarium, which will open in March 1999. I also have an extensive library at home, where I research topics in maritime history, archaeology, and oceanography that interest me and that relate to my work.

What is a normal working day like for you?

When you are working at sea, it is on a 24-hour basis. Your crew is standing three shifts of four hours on and eight hours off duty. As expedition leader, your job is to be awake, alert, and ready to make important decisions anytime, day or night. When it gets hot and heavy, you learn to survive on little sleep. You learn to catnap under all kinds of conditions.

Do you have any children? Is your family involved in your work?

I have had three boys and a girl. My oldest died in a car accident when he was 20. More and more, I hope to use a technology called telepresence that will allow me to continue my explorations from my home, with my family participating, instead of from a rolling deck. With telepresence a person can travel in half a second to remote locations and experience discoveries firsthand that now are limited to only a few people.

A close-up view of tube worms in the Gulf of Mexico

Clustered around hydrothermal vents in the Galápagos Rift, in the Pacific Ocean, these blood-red tube worms can grow to be eight feet tall.

What special preparations do you have to make for your work?

I need to assemble a dedicated team who shares my passion and has the knowledge and motivation to operate extremely complex technologies under the worst of conditions.

What is the hardest part of your work?

The hardest thing about my work is to convince people to sponsor an expedition—finding a Queen Isabella who'll hock her jewels and trust in my dream.

The "unsinkable" R.M.S. *Titanic* prepares to sail. One-way fare for the finest suite on the luxury liner would have cost $50,000 in today's dollars. A pocket watch found on the body of a *Titanic* victim shows water stains; the watch stopped just before 2 a.m. The ship sank at 2:20.

What was your biggest discovery? What are you most proud of?

My biggest discovery was the luxury liner *Titanic*, in the North Atlantic, but I am most proud of discovering hydrothermal vents and ancient Roman trading ships.

The hydrothermal vents, deep-sea hot springs that are formed when plates of earth move apart on the ocean floor and crack open in the crust, support truly amazing communities of undersea animals. Most of the creatures my colleagues and I found were completely new to science. We stored specimens in everything from Tupperware to plastic bags to take back for study.

I am proud to have the opportunity to bring history alive and to add to our scientific understanding. My expeditions are very careful to preserve our discoveries for research. We are not interested in treasure hunting. For example, we felt it was important not to diminish the *Titanic*'s beauty and dignity by taking objects from it.

What is left for you to explore?

My next project is one that National Geographic is sponsoring on the Battle of Midway. Right now I'm heavily involved with the research for this project and with assembling my team. Then, using a nuclear submarine that can go 3,000 feet below the surface—and hover or move along the ocean floor on special tires for more than a month—I plan to search for ancient shipwrecks in the eastern Mediterranean.

Finding at least one shipwreck from each century would provide such a fascinating, complete historical panorama. I plan to spend the next several years searching the deep sea for lost pages in our ancient history, stories locked in the cold, dark depths of Davy Jones's locker. All told, I've completed 110 expeditions, with 5 scheduled in 1998 and 3 more already scheduled for 1999.

In a painting by Ken Marschall, *Alvin's* lights glow on the *Titanic's* deck as the research vessel's robotic companion, *Jason Jr.*, examines the starboard anchor.

The JASON Project

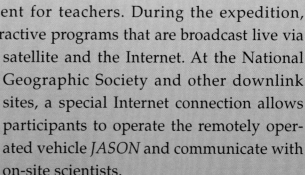

After discovering the wreck of the *Titanic*, world-famous explorer Dr. Robert Ballard received thousands of letters from students around the world wanting to go with him on his next expedition. He founded the JASON Project in 1989 to bring the thrill of discovery to millions of students worldwide.

The JASON Project is a year-round scientific expedition designed to excite and engage students in science and technology and to motivate and provide professional development for teachers. During the expedition, students can take part in real interactive programs that are broadcast live via satellite and the Internet. At the National Geographic Society and other downlink sites, a special Internet connection allows participants to operate the remotely operated vehicle *JASON* and communicate with on-site scientists.

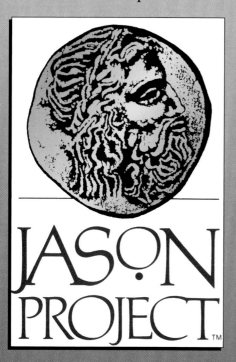

Find out more:
www.jasonproject.org

Michael L. Blakey

ANTHROPOLOGIST
Birthday: February 23, 1953

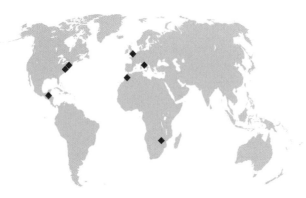

When I was a child I enjoyed playing games with my family and friends, but there were a lot of times when I liked to do things by myself. It was always great fun to visit my grandparents in the country. When I was about ten, I would explore the fields and woods with my brothers and cousins. We loved to pretend that we were great adventurers, finding new lands and streams, naming them, and even building little shelters where we created whole societies of our own.

My favorite thing to do was to hunt for arrowheads with my great uncle Kermit Mosely in rural Delaware. Native Americans lived in Delaware before the Europeans came and drove them out, and they left stone tools and bits of pottery behind. Uncle Kermit knew where to look for these artifacts, and he had a big collection of beautiful spears, axes, knives, arrowheads, and stone ornaments. I liked to walk through the fields with my eyes on the ground, dreaming about what the world was like when the Algonquins, who were my mother's ancestors, lived on this land.

I collected all kinds of things. When my parents took us camping, I would sometimes find small fossilized animals that were millions of years old. When I was very little, I caught insects in our backyard in Washington, D.C. But collecting was only the first part of the fun.

I next found books with pictures of the artifacts, fossils, or insects I had collected so I could read and learn about them. It was exciting to find a description of the same tool or bug that I had in my hand, like discovering it all over again.

In junior high I looked forward to the annual science fair and would always make an exhibit with either the Native American artifacts that I found with Uncle Kermit or with the fossils I collected with a friend on the cliffs of the Chesapeake Bay in Maryland. The first two years I won honorable mention, and then, in my third year, I won the grand prize. One of my science teachers helped me join an amateur archaeological club near my home, and on some weekends I helped dig at a local archaeological site like a real professional.

In high school I spent less time collecting and more time playing guitar and learning about African and African-American cultures. I went to Howard University in Washington, D.C., intending to study the guitar and become a composer. But an archaeology course brought back all of my childhood joy and fascination with studying artifacts and cultures that were hundreds, thousands, and even millions of years old. I was so excited that I studied hard and made better grades than ever before. During my junior year I had an opportunity to conduct an archaeological dig in the forests of Belize, in Central America. I mapped ancient Maya villages that archaeologists had never mapped before.

I will always be interested in archaeology, but I decided my senior year in college that I would understand cultures better if I studied the remains of the biology of the people themselves. I also liked learning about the different cultures of living people, so I decided to become an all-around anthropologist who could study human beings in many different ways.

Graduate school at the University of Massachusetts at Amherst was great fun because nearly all my courses were in anthropology. I also took some special courses at London and Oxford Universities, where I conducted research on the biology of living people in London. After seven years of graduate school, I had a Ph.D. in anthropology and became a professor at Howard University, where I teach and conduct research today.

What was the job that got you started in your field?

After ninth grade, my father helped me find a summer job studying Native American skeletons at the Smithsonian Institution with Dr. Donald Ortner, a great anthropologist. I studied 50 skulls that were hundreds of years old and found that the Pueblo people had many cavities from eating so much corn, but the Suroque people of Florida, mostly oyster-eaters, had few. Learning and dreaming about how these people lived was fun, although it meant taking lots of boring measurements. That summer I went to a lecture by one of my heroes, Dr. Louis Leakey. It was great. I shook his hand afterward, and he gave me his autograph.

What was the scariest thing that ever happened in your work?

My work can be dangerous, but it does not have to be. Traveling the world and visiting out-of-the-way places have their challenges. I have gotten into and out of enough tricky situations to believe that there are always solutions. If you are busy finding solutions, you do not have much time left to be scared of failure.

I do have one senseless fear, however: snakes. I do not like snakes. So, of course, the scariest thing that ever happened to me involved a big snake. I was 24 years old, mapping a new archaeological site in Corozal, Belize, and alone in the forest. Well, alone except for an eight-foot-long, aggressive, highly venomous snake called a yellow jaw, or fer-de-lance. I was in her home.

Now, a male and female yellow jaw live together in one place most of their lives. As a crew of Belizeans and I were clearing underbrush to make camp, we encountered a yellow jaw and killed him. For the month I was alone, I was on the lookout for his "wife." I had to kill her or constantly worry about an attack when I was not looking. When I saw her in a pile of sticks I had cut, it took all of my courage to go after her, but I was too slow and she got away.

My last day of this difficult expedition, I walked down the little picado, or path, to the coast, laughing that it would be my luck to get bitten by the yellow jaw that day. Just then I heard birds cawing and looked up to see two large, beautiful tropical birds in the trees, making quite a fuss. Not watching where I was

Mark Mack, Lab Director of the African Burial Ground Project, digs into history at the site in New York City.

"Nothing important is done in the short term or alone."

Michael Blakey

Blakey with archaeologist Theresa Singleton at the Granary of the Great Zimbabwe ruins, in Africa, in 1995

going, I stumbled, then looked down the path and saw the huge snake crossing just a few feet ahead of me. I stood frozen for what seemed to be a very long time while she pulled her full length across the picado. Then she was gone!

How do you choose a project?

I consider at least three factors: Does a project interest me; does it involve work I can do well; and does it study things that need to be better understood to help people solve serious problems? If it combines all three things, I get very excited.

I write out five-year plans with projects I want to do, and though I don't follow them step-by-step, they help me keep priorities in mind. I am amazed by how much gets done, even with goals set so high they seem like dreams to most people.

I read a lot of history about anthropologists, African-American scholars and activists, and the world in general. History affects my approach to projects, since it shows me the successes and failures of those who have gone before. A scholar is part of a long chain of thinkers who pass information from generation to generation. It is a privilege to be part of that chain, and it is important to me to return the favor by doing as much good as I can with what I learn.

Where do you work?

My work can take me anywhere people have been, from a laboratory in an old Italian castle to a laboratory in the casbah in Tangier, Morocco; from London to the Smithsonian's National Museum of Natural History. Now, at the W. Montague Cobb Biological Anthropology Laboratory, which I helped build at Howard University, I study the more than 1,000 human skeletons in the Cobb collection, including ones from my work on the African Burial Ground Project.

Blakey works with students in Howard University's Cobb Laboratory.

What is a normal working day like for you?

Every day is different. Two times a week I teach a course called Biology and Culture. I look in on the research staff working on the African Burial Ground Project to see that the bones are cleaned, reconstructed, measured, assessed, and photographed and that data are recorded correctly. African Americans especially care about our study of their ancestors, and I often speak to community groups and students. I read scientific journals daily and write about new facts we discover. I still go out looking for new archaeological sites once or twice a year.

Do you have any children? Is your family involved in your work?

My wife, Cecelie, and I have a five-year-old boy, Tariq, named after the African who conquered Spain in A.D. 711. He likes to visit my lab and see the skulls he calls "skeleton heads." I talk over ideas with Cecelie, whose useful comments on my papers make them read more clearly. She has degrees in African-American studies and in law, and a long career as a political activist, so her advice is valuable. She says she decided to marry me because she liked one of my papers.

What special preparations do you have to make for your work?

On field trips, I need sturdy clothes to keep me dry and a cap to block the sun. I take a shoulder bag with mapping instruments like a compass and a GPS (global positioning system), a hand-held device that picks up satellite signals to tell you where you are on the map. I carry a machete, a Swiss Army knife, a magnifying glass, a brush, dental tools, and a trowel for excavating. A pocket knife is particularly handy, not only because it is a great all-around tool, but because, in a jam, it can easily be traded for a few dollars or a favor anywhere in the world.

I use calipers to measure bones in the laboratory, and I use a laptop computer everywhere. And although I can map a site alone, it helps to have at least one other person. A thorough excavation or lab analysis takes six or more people.

What is the hardest part of your work?
I love my work. I do not think of any of it as hard.

What was your biggest discovery? What are you most proud of?
The African Burial Ground is one of the country's biggest archaeological projects. Its location in New York City was known to historians; now, through research on the more than 400 skeletons and artifacts found, I'm helping to discover its scientific and historic importance. People from Ghana and other African societies were captured, enslaved, and brought to New York before and during the Revolutionary War. We've learned that these ancestors of today's African Americans worked extremely hard to build and maintain the city, living in conditions so bad that nearly half of the children died.

The site was nearly destroyed by thoughtless people who wanted to build over it. Many African Americans were saddened to think their ancestors' cemetery would be treated with so little respect. I am very proud to help preserve part of the cemetery. In the year 2000 a monument and educational center will be built on the site to prevent us from ever forgetting our past.

What is left for you to explore?
There's no limit. We've barely scratched the surface of an understanding of the human past, present, and future. Everyone must bring his or her own point of view to this study, for there is always a need to re-examine old knowledge with new eyes.

Blakey found that enslaved Africans were worked so hard that nearly half died by the age of 12.

Ann Bowles

BIOACOUSTICIAN
Birthday: July 19, 1956

I got my Ph.D. in marine biology from the Scripps Institution of Oceanography, and I've been working at the Hubbs-Sea World Research Institute in San Diego, California, since 1979.

People always ask me how I managed to get my job ("You're so-o-o lucky!"). Mostly, I was lucky in my choice of parents. In the scientific heyday that followed the 1957 International Geophysical Year, my dad helped build a radio telescope in the desert outside Lima, Peru. My family moved there from Boulder, Colorado, when I was four years old. We traveled all over South America, and I still get little flashes of memory from this period, mental photographs to go with the real photos my dad took: pictures of me trying to catch big, metallic-blue morpho butterflies with my fingers; me sneaking up on a llama to see if it would really spit at me; me wandering off into the wilderness by myself; me smuggling a gigantic tadpole across the Andes in the family water cooler.

I always knew that I wanted to go into the sciences. I guess I must have picked that up from my dad. When I was growing up, I loved figuring out how to do little science projects. I viewed an eclipse though a pinhole in a piece of paper, built a sundial, learned how to make natural dyes with vegetables and vinegar—stuff like that. Some time during the seventh grade, I became a big fan of *Star Trek*. I realized that if I ever wanted to be a space explorer, I would need technical skills; so I made myself take remedial math and lots of science. I would not be working on marine mammals like I am today if I hadn't had that particular fantasy.

I was good at languages in high school, so I went on to study linguistics at the University of California, San Diego. I also took calculus, physics, biochemistry, and inorganic chemistry, all the while thinking, What does a linguist need with this stuff? I guess my instincts were better than I knew, because it turns out that I have used material from every course I took.

When I was finishing college, though, I realized there was a problem— linguists have to work with humans all the time. I like anything that wiggles except humans. So, during my last two years of college, I decided to use what I had learned about human communication to study animal communication instead. To get my Ph.D. I had to write a thesis, which described research I had done on individual vocal recognition in the emperor penguin.

Nowadays, most of my day-to-day work involves helping solve the problems that arise as people take their snowmobiles, Jet Skis, aircraft, and industry into wilderness areas. In the course of my career, I have studied the effects of human-made noise on marine mammals like California sea lions, elephant seals, dolphins, and humpback whales; desert animals like kangaroo rats, kit foxes, and desert tortoises; domesticated wildlife like ostriches, emus, and rheas; and beautiful, ancient leatherback sea turtles.

When people ask what my favorite animal is, I have to make up something on the spot—I have been enchanted by every species in turn.

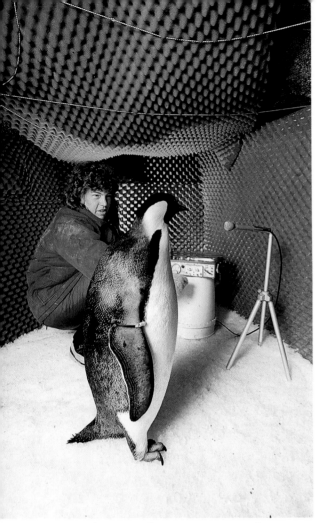

Bowles records emperor penguin calls in a quiet studio set up in the otherwise noisy Penguin Encounter at Hubbs-Sea World.

What was the job that got you started in your field?

I got into my particular specialty by pure accident. I started volunteering at Hubbs-Sea World because, like many young people then, I wanted to study dolphin language. When I arrived, the director, Bill Evans, gave me "The Lecture" that all marine mammalogists give to every wanna-be dolphin scientist. He told me I'd be crazy to study dolphins. "But," he said, "Sea World has nice penguins." That is how I began studying penguin calls and why I went to the Antarctic Peninsula.

I had to eat while doing my thesis, so I worked as a research assistant on a study of the effects of space shuttle sonic booms on pinnipeds (seals and sea lions) in the California Channel Islands. I got the job because I knew how to use a spectrograph, a machine that makes voice prints. While doing this project, I realized that a lot of interesting questions are hidden in the seemingly mundane study of noise effects, and I've been asking these questions ever since.

What was the scariest thing that ever happened in your work?

When you think of scary, you probably think of physical danger, but scientists take pride in designing their studies so that no one will ever get hurt. Instead, science is full of emotional danger. For example, to qualify for my thesis I had to take an oral exam, answering questions put to me by some of the most famous people in my field. These tests are supposed to turn your brain inside out, but I felt like they removed my brain entirely and then kicked me in the stomach.

Even now, years later, I remember many of the questions perfectly. When Theodore Bullock, a very famous neurophysiologist, asked me why birds sing, I fumbled through an idiotic, scientific-sounding answer, and he laughed. "No," he said, "they do it because they feel like it." It sounded like a joke, but I later realized what he meant. Whether we realize it or not, our natural drives shape our behavior. This lesson has guided my work ever since.

How do you choose a project?

I like projects that help me discover general principles that describe the impact that humans have on all animals. I try to find the best animal to help answer a particular question—sometimes that means working on kangaroo rats instead of dolphins.

Where do you work?

Beyond Hubbs-Sea World, my place of work varies depending on the animals I am studying. My work has taken me from the Mojave Desert to islands in the sub-Antarctic, from the Perené River in Peru to the cloud forests of northern California.

What is a normal working day like for you?

By nature I am a night person, so "normal working day" is not quite right in my case. I tend to get up late in the morning and stay up way late. I have always tried to work on animals with convenient circadian rhythms; that is, animals whose daily rhythm of activities is compatible with mine. One of my favorite professors, Jack Bradbury, taught me this trick. He advised his students to work on ground squirrels because they never get up before ten in the morning and they go to bed at four in the afternoon!

Do you have any children? Is your family involved in your work?

I tend to think of the animals in my life as my family, and they are certainly involved in my work. For example, we have a little elephant seal who is learning to push a button when she hears a sound. Elephant seals are not the smartest animals in the world, but she is so sincere that no one minds waiting for her to figure things out.

Bowles with a pair of Hubbs-Sea World's killer whales

With her tape recorder protected from curious penguins by a screen, Bowles photographs the reaction to her playback of penguin calls.

What special preparations do you have to make for your work?

When I go into the field, I haul along more gear than any ten human beings ought to need: computers, cameras, video and audio recorders, community noise monitors, loudspeakers, Yagi antennas, GPS receivers, sonobuoys, and on and on. This behavior has cost me at least one relationship, but I can't help it— it's normal for bioacousticians.

What is the hardest part of your work?

I think the gut reaction of most scientists would be: "Ughh. Getting money is the hardest thing!!" For me, the hardest thing of all is watching helplessly while wild things get destroyed. Every time I see a new housing development going up, I remember chance meetings with scrub jays, and I miss them the way you would miss a friend who has died.

What was your biggest discovery? What are you most proud of?

In my field, there are no Jane Goodalls or Marie Curies who paved the way. My generation of women in bioacoustics will be the first to make discoveries that others look to in the future. It is hard to tell what these discoveries will be, though. Most real scientists don't get a big flash of light that you might call a moment of discovery. Instead, we build our intellectual adventures out of little steps.

"Live your life as though what you do affects every other living thing on earth."

Ann Bowles

Bowles gently measures a leatherback sea turtle's hearing in Trinidad.

My favorite example comes from my own study of the responses of desert tortoises to jet noise. Desert tortoises are charming animals whose warm, dry, wrinkled skin is very soft to the touch. Their faces are full of individual character. They are just like the little old village elders I met when I was a girl.

In 1995 my colleague Scott Eckert and I discovered that tortoises hear very well at summer temperatures, but they don't have an acoustic startle response—when a jet noise surprises them, their hearts don't beat fast and they don't jump. Instead, they freeze in place, sometimes with a foot suspended in midstep. I've seen them freeze for up to 113 minutes. I hope this little fact will change the way people perceive reptiles. Just because a tortoise doesn't jump, it doesn't mean it didn't react. Why does this matter? Well, if a tortoise freezes for long periods, there may be consequences—it may not get enough to eat, for example.

Domestic turkeys react to the noise of an airplane flying overhead.

What is left for you to explore?

For the rest of my career, I'd like to link all the little steps into a meaningful journey, one that will inspire people to understand and respect what I call the other earthlings— our animal neighbors. After that, I have a crazy dream that someone will donate about ten million dollars to our research institution, and I'll go off to the Falklands or Macquarie Island or Marion Island to study penguins and albatrosses for the rest of my life. It might not come true, but I can dream, can't I?

David Doubilet

UNDERWATER PHOTOGRAPHER
Birthday: November 28, 1946

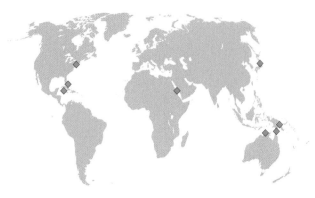

I grew up in New York City, a very strange place to go diving. When I was ten, my uncle took me to the premier of the movie *The Silent World—La Monde Silencieux*. Produced by Jacques Cousteau, the film was shot in the Red Sea and the Indian Ocean. I was absolutely mesmerized. Sometimes it happens to you. You see something—a moment, a part of life—that changes the course of your life. I was very lucky because it happened when I was ten.

After the film, knees trembling, I went up to Jacques Cousteau, who stood straight, tall, aloof and very French, talking to people in the theater. I sneaked between a forest of legs, looked up at him, pulled his jacket and said, "Oh, Captain Cousteau, I want to swim underwater and take pictures. I want to be an underwater photographer." He looked down and said, "Why not?"

My family spent summers at our house on the New Jersey shore. The sea there is dark and murky and changes all the time. Rough or calm, it is always green. That's where I began diving. I had a simple yellow face mask and green flippers from a company called Frankie the Frog Man. The flippers looked like lily pads. My snorkel was made of hard rubber that hurt my mouth, but I could put my head under and breathe when I swam. I learned to be a good free diver and how to spearfish, too, because that's what you did underwater in those days.

At 12, I learned to scuba dive using a double tank that was heavier than I was. I became a certified diver at 13. There was no formal certification then. There was a group called the New York Skin Diving Academy. I had to study the physics of diving. I learned about air embolisms, the bends, and even the history of diving. In 1956 the sport was barely 12 years old, so I was a young pioneer.

I liked to be underwater for one simple reason: I could escape the rest of the world. I could escape school or parents or lunch if I didn't like it. I was constantly being sought for something I was either late for, or forgot to do, or did not want to do in the first place. Being at the bottom of the pool was like being at the bottom of the ocean—no one could reach me.

My parents never really encouraged me, but they never discouraged me. Everyone in my family did different things. My father, a doctor, liked to fish; my mother played golf; one sister skied; my other sister ice-skated. Everything I did, I did on my own, and everything was possible. I learned early on that if you want to do something, you go and do it.

There were few books about underwater photography back then. I didn't know as much as the authors of those books, but I wasn't far behind. Using a rubber bag, I adapted my first camera, a Kodak Brownie Hawkeye, for underwater pictures. The first results were absolutely terrible, but I wasn't discouraged. I was taking pictures of everything: fish, mussels and clams, and people peering down from the surface of a swimming pool. I was shooting bubbles. At 14, I won my first photography contest. At 15, my picture of a diver pulling up an anchor sold to a South American magazine. My school did not offer photography courses like many schools do today. But even if you're a student, you can't say, "I want to make student pictures." You must say, "I want to make real pictures that will tell a story and please me."

Photography depends on light. How does the light look in the morning? What kind of shadow does a glass of juice cast? Einstein called photographers "light monkeys," because they are fooling with, playing with, and constantly moving the light. A photographer must be as aware of light as a perfume-maker is of smells.

Photography comes from the heart. Strangely enough, it's not something you do, but something you use to explore your interests and to translate them into images.

David Doubilet

Dinah Halstead, a dive guide and boat captain in Papua New Guinea, among a perfect circle of barracuda

What was the job that got you started in your field?

When I was 12, my father and I went to Andros, an island in the Bahamas, to a resort being started by a Canadian named Dick Birch. He took me diving and, impressed with my diving ability and knowledge of diving physics, he offered me a three-week job. After that I worked on Andros during the summers and eventually became a dive guide. At 16, I worked for the U.S. Fish and Wildlife Service at the Sandy Hook Marine Lab, in New Jersey, first as a volunteer, then as a paid summer worker. I worked with people like Dr. Ronald Eisler, who conducted the first experiment on how pollution affects marine fish. By 17, I was the chief photographer at the Sandy Hook Marine Lab.

What was the scariest thing that has ever happened in your work?

Scary happens when you don't plan, when there is a storm, when you're in deep water. I've been very deep, diving at the edge of whatever safe diving is. Once, at almost 250 feet, I was strongly affected by nitrogen narcosis, a condition that makes you lose peripheral vision, or the ability to see all the things around you. I was breathing very thick air because as you go deeper, the air compresses. Your lungs can't get enough nourishment, so it's as if you're choking. I swam toward the surface, but I wasn't getting any closer. Little by little the edges of my vision closed in like the iris of a camera. I was drowning; I was dying. Fortunately, my buddy caught me and dragged me up. I had been swimming along the face of a reef, instead of going up. Nitrogen narcosis produces a sudden vertigo, and you lose your sense of what's up or down; you lose direction and your concept of where you stand. That was scary.

Despite the fear they inspire, there are many more sharks eaten by people than there are people eaten by sharks.

Once, while photographing great white sharks in Australia, I was outside of the shark cage but kept my foot next to it so I could quickly get back in. It was a beautiful, clear day. Shafts of sunlight came through the surface. The white, sandy bottom with beautiful green seaweed and algae swaying was such a lovely picture that I lay down in the algae to get the shot. I started photographing a shark that was far away. I kept taking pictures as the shark drew closer, but it was becoming more and more agitated. Then I thought, Aha, it's time to get back into the cage. I looked around, but there was no cage.

A swell had lifted the boat, cage, and anchor, moving the whole business 50 yards away. I thought, Well, I'll just swim back, then remembered I wasn't wearing fins. So I started bouncing along the bottom, backward, backing up and pushing the shark away with my camera when he came close. I'd shove him hard at times, and he'd dart away, then come back for another pass. It was like a nightmare. Finally, I got to the cage. My friend pulled me inside and slammed the door. The shark was furious and smashed against the cage with his teeth. That was frightening. But it's not always so scary underwater. It's more beautiful than scary.

Doubilet photographed shark scientist Eugenie Clark using bait to lure a great white from inside the safety of her antishark cage.

Doubilet tests remote-control camera equipment underwater in the Red Sea.

"If you want to become a diver and a photographer, you have to trust your heart, your brain, and your interests. Learn about the visual world; spend time looking at art and how painters deal with light."

David Doubilet

How do you choose a project?

One story may lead to another. There's a place in the Red Sea where I've shot photographs for ten stories. I started there with a story on garden eels that live in the sand. Then my partner, Dr. Eugenie Clark, discovered a flounder that repels sharks by exuding a poison—that became our second story. After that we did a story about photoblepheron, a small black fish that lives in the area. These fish have pockets under their eyes that produce pools of light they use to hunt plankton at night. National Geographic has covered this area extensively, but new things are continually found.

Where do you work?

I spend as much time in the ocean as possible. My work has taken me all over the world. My real strength is looking at the coral reef system, and I have worked in many locations with temperate water. I've never gone to the North or South Pole to dive under the ice. I'd like to, but if I have a choice of cold or warm water, I'll pick warm water.

When at home, I research future story ideas, talk with publishers and editors about my books, give lectures, and prepare for the next underwater assignment.

What is a normal working day like for you?

My assistant in Australia, Gary Bell, and I start diving at nine or even earlier and spend up to six hours in the water. We break for meals. Sometimes we dive at night. We have up to ten cameras because we cannot change lenses or film underwater. Another assistant, Nicky Konstantino, and I have made many dives in Japan where we start deep, then stay a long time working our way up the cliff of a reef. It can take four hours, so we just dive once a day. We go deep for 30 minutes, and the rest of the time is spent in decompression, shooting all the time.

Do you have any children? Is your family involved in your work?

I met my wife, Anne, at college, and we've been diving partners ever since. She's a photographer, and we've done a lot of our assignments together. Our daughter, Emily, is, at 14, a certified diver, and she loves it. She may not be an underwater photographer when she grows up, but her experience with the ocean will certainly help her in life. On almost every vacation, we go diving as a family.

What special preparations do you have to make for your work?

Unless my job is near a big city—and most underwater sites are not—it can be a nightmare. Forgetting one thing is big trouble. Everything underwater is lit with electronic flash, so I need strobes and the arms to attach them to the camera's housing. It's not enough to corner a fish in a dark cave and blast him with a strobe. I must look at fish or coral or approaching sharks and think how to light them. I swim underwater like a giant spider crab with all my equipment.

Each bag I take contains one complete camera system with all the equipment and parts for the underwater housing of the camera. That way, if I lose one bag, which is my biggest fear, I won't be out of luck. This means, though, that I can end up with as many as 15 bags. And, of course, I have to take clothes, my diving gear, and my surface cameras.

I always carry my mask with my glasses on the plane. That's one thing I can't replace in the field. I can borrow a regulator or fins or a wet suit, but not a mask. I've worn the same mask for 25 years, a round rubber one that fits comfortably—just like the mask that Cousteau had. Mine has big glasses built in so I look a bit like Little Orphan Annie: wondrous and open-eyed.

A school of nine-lined sweetlips, caught in Doubilet's light, seems to be trying to mimic a much larger fish—possibly to confuse predators.

A Red Sea hawkfish

What's the hardest part of your work?

Packing. Hate it. Unpacking. Hate it. Lugging bags to the airport, boarding planes, paying overweight fees, going through Customs around the world. That's the hardest. I don't think I'll be eaten by a shark or drown in deep water. I think I'll have a heart attack or an internal explosion trying to get on a plane.

What was your biggest discovery? What are you most proud of?

I'm most proud of bringing a place like the Red Sea into the consciousness of people or making people aware of stingrays in the Cayman Islands. The stingrays get fed daily now and prosper. When the boats leave in the evening, the stingrays resume their normal behavior, snuffling in the sand for clams and shells.

In Western Australia we were the first to publicize a place where whale sharks were regular visitors. A story on night-feeding manta rays off Hawaii's

Emily Doubilet swims with stingrays in the Cayman Islands.

A year-old crocodile pauses for a sniff of air as it swims over a sandbar in Australia's Jardine River.

Kona Coast helped make it one of the most dynamic dive spots in the United States. A hundred people a night will go to see them. Now there are more manta rays there than I ever remembered.

What is left for you to explore?

I learn something with every dive. Humans have been underwater only about 50 years. Most of our planet is sea, yet we're just beginning to explore it. How old do fish get? How much coral do they eat? How does a reef change? What grows on what? We're making discoveries in places like Indonesia or New Guinea.

My work in the future may also help to show how fragile the sea is. The sea is the last place in the world where humans hunt for food, and although the fish in the sea seem endless, they are not. They cannot support the great hunger that humans have for them.

Most of all, I will continue to make the pictures that I love. There is a moment of life and light and time when it all comes together in a picture. That's the most joyous thing. I never, ever, go into the water without a camera. That almost includes showers and baths.

A 16-foot crocodile leaps from the Adelaide River in Australia hoping for a treat from a tour boat.

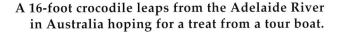

Jane Goodall

ETHOLOGIST
Birthday: April 3, 1934

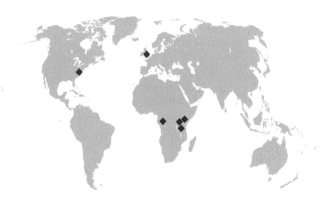

I have been interested in animals since before I can remember. From the time I was very small, I was fascinated with creepy, crawling, furry, flying creatures. When I was quite young, my mother found me in my room with a handful of worms in my bed, watching as they went around and around. She didn't say, "Yuk!" and throw them out the window. She said, "Jane, if you leave them in here, they'll die. They need the air." And so I let them go free.

In fact, my mother is the most important reason for my doing what I've done and being who I've been. When I was four years old, I stayed on a farm, where I helped collect hens' eggs. I became puzzled and asked those around me, "Where is the hole big enough for the eggs to come out?" When no one answered to my satisfaction, I hid in a small, stuffy henhouse for four hours to find out. While I watched and waited, my mother looked frantically for me in the house and garden. She even called the police to help locate me. But when my mother saw me rushing toward the house in excitement, she didn't scold me for disappearing for so long. She sat down and listened to me tell the wonderful story of how a hen lays eggs.

Even my first books were about animals. I read *The Story of Dr. Doolittle, The Jungle Book,* and *Tarzan.* Looking back, I see that the original Tarzan was terribly hard on animals. But I didn't realize it then. Books are a great source of inspiration. They lure your mind to be imaginative. By the time I was eight or nine, I was dreaming of going to Africa. And my mother, a very special person, would say, "Jane, if you really want something and if you work hard, take advantage of opportunities, and never give up, you will somehow find a way."

In those days you had to learn a foreign language to get a scholarship to a university. But I couldn't do it—I couldn't speak French, couldn't speak German, couldn't speak Latin. So Mum said, "Why not take a secretarial course, then you can get a job anywhere in the world." So that's what I did.

But that didn't lead me directly to Africa. After I finished my secretarial class I began working for a documentary film company—a wonderful job, but with very low pay. When a school friend invited me to visit her family in Kenya, I readily accepted. I quit my job with the film company to begin work as a waitress in order to save the money. Finally, at age 23, with only enough money for boat fare to Africa (that was the cheapest way to travel in those days), I went off by myself to an unknown continent.

After two months in Africa I met the man who made all my dreams come true. Louis Leakey was an anthropologist and paleontologist who was interested in animals and early man. I made an appointment to meet him. Because I had studied animals throughout my childhood, I was able to answer many of his questions about the natural world, and he gave me a job as his assistant. I traveled with Louis and his wife, Mary, on one of their fossil-hunting expeditions to Olduvai Gorge. After some time, Louis decided I was the person he had been looking for to study the chimpanzees living near the shore of Lake Tanganyika, in what is now called Tanzania. And when the British authorities refused to let a young, untrained girl venture into the wilds of Africa on her own, who should volunteer to accompany me for the first three months but my own amazing mother.

And so my work began. After several years in Africa I returned to England to work for my Ph.D. in ethology from Cambridge University, and then I returned to the paradise of Gombe Stream, Tanzania, to continue my research.

Jane Goodall

What was the job that got you started in your field?

When I arrived in Kenya at age 23, I heard about Dr. Louis Leakey and went to see him. He took me around the natural history museum, asking me about animals in the exhibits and dropping words like "ichthyologist," to see if I understood them. I'd read so much about Africa and gone to so many museums that I could answer many of his questions, so Dr. Leakey offered me a job. The work included a trip to Olduvai Gorge, and based on what I did there, Dr. Leakey felt that I was the one he wanted to study chimpanzees.

I learned that you might not reach your goal directly, but if you hang on you'll find a way. If it's worth it, it's worth waiting for. It's so important to be prepared. That is why I worked to get my university degree, and why my studies were so disciplined. You may have to force yourself to sit and do the work, but in time it becomes fascinating, too.

"If you really want to do something, and work hard enough, and take advantage of opportunity, and never give up, you'll find a way. Follow your dreams. If you really want to do something, don't let anybody tell you that you can't."

Jane Goodall

Young Flint reaches out to Goodall.

What was the scariest thing that ever happened in your work?

When the chimps stopped fearing me, they became aggressive and wanted me to leave. They are much stronger than I am, and when a big male chimp charges at you, yelling, it is very frightening. Recently, Frodo, the biggest chimp we've ever had, 115 pounds of solid muscle, began bullying people. One time he grabbed my ankles and pulled me down a hill. He's calmer now, thank goodness.

Once, to observe monkeys on an island in Lake Victoria, I had to go through a tunnel used by hippos. As I was trying to reach the beach where they played, I heard footsteps but had nowhere to go. Edging back into the dense undergrowth, I peered out and saw a crocodile poacher with a great long spear. I didn't like the looks of him, but knowing he was bound to see me, I thought it best to warn him I was there. I stepped out onto the path toward him, and he, startled, raised his arm and pointed his spear right at me. That was probably the most frightening thing that ever happened. Later, realizing I was harmless, he moved away.

Goodall and friend romp with the chimps at Tchimpounga Sanctuary, in the Congo.

How do you choose a project?

When I hear of chimps in need, in the wild or in captivity, I try to help. To raise money for my projects I sometimes give lectures and make appeals. Meanwhile, our research teams are in the field, monitoring chimps we have identified and known for a while. In the wild chimps can live 40 to 50 years; in captivity they may live to be 60. We follow the different individuals. Every one has a unique life history.

We may observe an infant and its mother, or males squabbling over dominance. We may also have the opportunity to observe a mother with twins or to observe an orphan adopted by a male. Such events are rare, and we may never see them again. There are still so many questions.

Where do you work?

It's unusual for me to be in one place for long. The longest I've been anywhere since 1986 is three weeks. Usually I'm traveling, living out of suitcases and sharing information about the chimps, about the dangers to the natural world, and about what people can do to help.

Orphaned chimps make fast friends at Tchimpounga Sanctuary.

What is a normal working day like for you?

In the field, every morning I would climb to my special peak with my binoculars, and a flashlight if needed, so I'd be ready when the chimps awoke. I recorded what I saw, sometimes even climbing into the treetops, whether I saw a chimp or not. It was marvelous. If it rained, I covered myself with a sheet of polyethylene. Sometimes it was very cold. I got extremely thin. When you follow the chimps, they may go through thick, thorny, viney places. I often stopped to look at things because everything interests me, not just chimpanzees. You're in a magic world and if you rush through it, you lose it.

At times, a photographer or filmmaker joined me, but I usually went alone to observe the chimps quietly. Alone with the chimps, you can forget about humans. It's important not to disturb what the chimpanzees are doing because then you won't see them as they really are. I did try eating their food: fruit, leaves, and even insects. We do help if the chimps get sick. One chimpanzee, Gilka, allowed me to put antibiotics on her infected hand. If we seem non-threatening, then for the most part, the chimps will learn to trust us.

When I stay for three weeks at my home in England, I get up at 5:30 a.m. to get as much work done as I can. I eat breakfast, take the dog out, fix lunch, and have all afternoon for writing—books, letters, reports. I spend time with my family in the evening and then write late into the night.

Do you have any children? Is your family involved in your work?

When my son was born, I felt I'd learned a lot from the chimps about being a mother. I learned that it can be such fun. We had enormous fun. My son's name is Hugo, but his nickname is Grub. He was with me in Africa for his first nine years, then lived with my mother during his term time in England. Living in the Serengeti, surrounded by lions and hyenas, we kept an eye on Grub all the time. He grew up with my work but didn't get interested in it. He now lives in Tanzania, speaks Kiswahili, and is very African in his outlook.

When I first started my research, my mother joined me for the first three months in Tanzania because British authorities wouldn't allow me to be on my own. She's still tremendously involved in my work. My sister came to help with photographs in the early days. And Grub's father, Hugo van Lawick, filmed hours of chimpanzee behavior in the early days as well.

What special preparations do you have to make for your work?

I used to go out into the field with a tape recorder and a pencil and paper. When I began my research, everything was new and I had to develop my own research methods. I had very little money in the early days. I took few clothes and ate very simply. I had curiosity, patience, and persistence. I was incredibly fit; not eating or drinking all day didn't bother me. And I always told someone roughly the direction I was going.

What is the hardest part of your work?

Getting funding is difficult. In the field, it's physically demanding to stay with the chimps and record information. You don't feel like getting up at 5 a.m. to go through a horrible thorny tangle, but you must follow the research plan you've set for yourself. Moreover, collecting data is fun, but you need it in a form you can analyze. You follow one individual all day and write details of his or her behavior, and then analyze the day later. It took a strong sense of self-discipline to go out, seven days a week, rain or shine or feeling ill. When I was in Kigoma, Tanzania, the British living there were shocked and said, "You must take Sunday off." I'd love to check my notes to see what I learned on Sundays!

Analyzing data is much harder than collecting it. But then even after seeing something a hundred times, you may suddenly realize: That's why they do it! It's a breakthrough. You light up inside. It's another kind of discovery.

At dusk Goodall awaits another night of observation.

When Goodall began in 1960, she thought her research might take three years. Continuing what has become the world's longest field study of animals, she patiently writes up her notes under a protective mosquito net.

What was your biggest discovery? What are you most proud of?

The most exciting discovery in the early days was finding that chimps used tools, because it was thought that only humans were toolmakers.

I'm most proud of something quite different. Through the observations of the chimps and subsequent studies, people's attitude toward non-human animals has definitely begun to change. There is no question that this change, among scientists and ordinary people alike, is because chimps are so like us.

Also, because I didn't subscribe to the scientific thinking of the time, I gave chimps names and not numbers. I talked about their personalities at a time when only humans were believed to have personalities. I also described their minds and emotions, both believed to be uniquely human. I saw their minds as human-type minds. Early on, my thinking had been affected by my dog, Rusty. His behavior taught me that animals have minds and human-like emotions.

What is left for you to explore?

The most exciting thing for future chimp studies is finding out how the different populations or communities across Africa vary. There are cultural variations. The sad thing is that, even as we speak, whole communities are being destroyed, so we will never learn how flexible their behavior is. We'll never learn about all of their different cultures, because many have already gone.

Roots & Shoots

Roots & Shoots is the Jane Goodall Institute's program for young people. It emphasizes the value of each individual and inspires and encourages members—from kindergarten to university level—to play their part in making the world around them a better place. Each group tackles at least three projects that show care and concern—for the environment, for animals, and for the human community.

You can make a difference by joining or starting a Roots & Shoots club in your area.

Find out more:
The Jane Goodall Institute
Roots & Shoots Director
P.O. Box 14890
Silver Spring, MD 20911

CHIMPANZOO

CHIMPANZOO is an international research project dedicated to the study of chimpanzees in zoos and other captive settings. Trained by local zoo personnel and the Jane Goodall Institute, caretakers, students, and volunteers gather behavioral data for comparative studies and to provide the chimpanzees with more enriching environments. The CHIMPANZOO office can let you know how you can become involved.

Find out more:
CHIMPANZOO Director
Geronimo Bldg., Room #308
800 E. University Blvd.
Tucson, AZ 85721

Dereck & Beverly Joubert

WILDLIFE FILMMAKERS
Dereck's birthday: March 3, 1956
Beverly's birthday: January 12, 1957

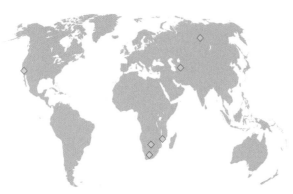

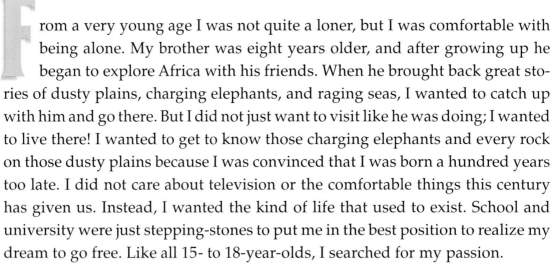

Dereck's Story

From a very young age I was not quite a loner, but I was comfortable with being alone. My brother was eight years older, and after growing up he began to explore Africa with his friends. When he brought back great stories of dusty plains, charging elephants, and raging seas, I wanted to catch up with him and go there. But I did not just want to visit like he was doing; I wanted to live there! I wanted to get to know those charging elephants and every rock on those dusty plains because I was convinced that I was born a hundred years too late. I did not care about television or the comfortable things this century has given us. Instead, I wanted the kind of life that used to exist. School and university were just stepping-stones to put me in the best position to realize my dream to go free. Like all 15- to 18-year-olds, I searched for my passion.

I knew that I wanted to be on the mystical plains of Africa, and I got a job there as a guide. One day a male lion that I was tracking suddenly charged at me, very nearly killing me. He stopped just in front of me, and as I looked into those fierce yellow eyes, I suddenly released all my fear. I wanted to touch him. I wanted to enjoy every second of the moment, and more important, to share that moment with everyone. I started photography to be able to share, to talk to people with a common experience. No one has exactly the same feeling when looking at an image, but everyone who sees a dramatic image and is captivated by it somehow shares a common conspiracy of emotions.

My career choices would not have been possible without the support and understanding of the people I love and who love me. When I decided to leave the city to live in Africa, I took a deep breath and approached my father. He had high hopes for me having an accounting or law career. I told him that I was going to live in the bush. Quietly he said, "What took you so long to decide? I've seen it coming for years. You haven't chosen the easiest life, but good luck!"

And then there was Beverly. We met in high school, and after a one-year stint in the military for me, we began dating. Beverly, besides being beautiful and bright, was the only girl I had ever met who was not into the things I considered trivial that occupy the minds of many teenagers. I could talk to her about non-dating-related topics—so we courted! We made plans to finish our education and carve a life out of nothing. We decided on the life we wanted to have and then found a way to make it work for us. So we live in a tent under a tree on land that belongs to no one. We do not have a television or a bathtub. I never wear a suit and tie, and Beverly never has to sit and chat about the latest microwave. We're equal partners in an adventure of a lifetime, and we have a view of the world that most people think exists only in documentaries on television.

Zebra-striped capes help camouflage the Jouberts' movements as they work.

Beverly's Story

When I was growing up, my parents always enjoyed taking us on vacation to the great wildlife sanctuaries of South Africa, Zimbabwe, and Mozambique. I remember both enjoying the experience and disliking the restriction of having to see it through a car window. I wanted to be out there. My family loved camping, so the outdoors always appealed to me. I started to document our trips and the family life with photographs that I took.

Throughout school I felt misunderstood. My teachers tried to pigeonhole me as something I did not want to be. In truth, I did not know what I wanted to do with my life except experience it—travel, explore, and soak it all up before assuming a role that I did not want and that would make me unhappy. It was more subconscious, really, but I knew I was saving myself for something quite different and special.

Throughout my childhood, my parents always had a ton of pets: my mother once had 18 cats, 2 or 3 dogs, and at least 50 birds. Stray animals would arrive at our home and never leave. My twin brother, Brian, and I were tearabouts, constantly together, poking our fingers into spider holes or climbing up to birds' nests. So I was well prepared and, in some ways, an open canvas when I met Dereck. His passion to live in the bush was evident from day one.

I could do that, I realized. Because of my constant companionship with my brother, Brian, I had learned how to be with someone all the time. In the bush there is often no escape. You are with your partner 24 hours a day, and if you are a sulky lone wolf or a gregarious party animal, it can be rough on your partner. At first, though, it was difficult for me to find a creative role, because it is still a man's world, especially in Africa. Dereck coached me on using his 35-mm still cameras, and I jumped at the opportunity. Eventually, I took over all of the still photography for our operation. I engulfed myself in the natural sounds of the bush and started to enjoy and record them, and this started my career in the film industry.

In this career, as in so much else, I found a soul mate in Dereck. I had always wanted to explore before settling down. We found that exploring is way more fun than settling down, so we never did. Society needs both the people who find comfort in a life of stability and responsibility and the exploring "scouts of the world." I do not feel that what we do is somehow more valid than the work of a bank teller. Our life is simply what we enjoy; many would not like it.

Beverly Joubert

"If you have a passion for something, follow it. So many people waste their lives in meaningless, boring jobs, living in fear because they are afraid of believing in their passion."

Dereck Joubert

What was the job that got you started in your field?

DERECK: I started off by going to university to study geology and ecology. **BEVERLY:** I started off at business college and in catering. We both worked at a game lodge in a game reserve, managing the lodge together. Dereck became a ranger as well. The game reserve is where we began our experience with animals. To be able to make films, you have to know and understand the subjects you are filming as much as you must know how to make a film.

Working nights on a film with Boyd Matson

A lion cub playfully practices a neck bite that will be deadly to its prey in a few years.

What was the scariest thing that ever happened in your work?

DERECK: Danger is definitely a part of daily life. Lions have charged us and walked around our tents at night; elephants have smashed our truck over and over; and we've had scorpion stings, malaria, and a host of other illnesses. But that is what makes our lives adventurous, fun, and worth living. I'd be bored silly without these things.

BEVERLY: We have modified our lives to live closely to the natural environment and usually do not have major confrontations with the animals, since we do not threaten them at all. I remember one experience very clearly when an elephant caught us totally by surprise. At the time we had no fear because we had to stay calm to survive, but afterward, I remember shaking like a leaf.

An elephant cow charged us one day, coming straight out of the river from behind some reeds. Just the slight metallic sound of us getting out of the vehicle had alerted her. When we saw her, we returned to our vehicle to start filming the herd. She began to charge at us, and even though we stood our ground, she continued. We were in an open vehicle with no windshield, doors, or roof. She held her head low and attacked from the front, putting her whole head on the hood. She was so close we could have touched her tusks.

She hit the vehicle a few times, lifting it, and then pushed us backward at quite a speed toward a huge hole in the ground. Dereck put his foot on the brake, and the elephant caught her tusks on the bush bar, which protects the vehicle's radiator. She jerked her head up, breaking off a tip of one of her tusks. She stopped to feel the tip of her tusk with her trunk and then walked away, leaving us alone. As she walked off, we saw a huge wound under her belly. We thought that she had been wounded by poachers, which is what made her so startled by the slight noise we made getting out of the vehicle.

The main danger for us in the bush is the poacher. Poachers are totally out of control. Greed keeps them killing animals, and if we got in the way, they would not hesitate to kill us, too.

How do you choose a project?

We always go with something we both feel passionate about. This is not a job; it is a lifestyle that keeps us out of mischief and earns us money. So we simply do not take on a project that we do not feel really excited or good about. Living in the bush helps us choose our projects as they unfold right out in front of us. Most of the time we feel so strongly about a conservation problem that we take on a film to help change the situation. If we just took on anything to get paid, we really would not be fair to ourselves, the project, to whoever was paying for it, or those who watch it.

Where do you work?

We almost always work in Africa in the bush with big, dangerous animals like lions, elephants, buffaloes, or hippos, because we believe that if we can get people to pay attention to the big stuff, then we are a step closer to saving the smaller animals. As a result, we live and work a 7-hour drive away—over the worst sand roads—from the nearest village of 600 people, and an 18-hour drive away from Johannesburg, in South Africa, our main supply center. To get a pint of milk, we have to drive 7 hours; so we go without! There is nowhere we will not go if it is wild. We went to Siberia to find tigers, to Turkmenistan to find snow leopards, and to Mozambique to dive for dugongs. The great thing is that we get to do these things as a job!

The Jouberts get up close in Chobe National Park, in Botswana.

While filming *Into Africa*, the Jouberts and Boyd Matson sit near a water hole popular with elephants.

What is a normal working day like for you?

Our day is dictated by animal behavior, there is no normal day. One day we might be up at one or two in the morning following lions. Another day we'll sleep in (until 5 a.m.!) then go looking for elephants. Most days we start by tracking an animal we want to work with, and most days we are lucky. We find lions, for example, and then the real work begins.

We set up the cameras and wait. We polish our lenses and clean the equipment. The worst thing that can happen is to have a camera jam during a great scene, so the equipment is always clean. We eat and wait. Drink water and wait. Watch the lions and wait. Then suddenly they will be up running, hunting, killing something. If we have done our job well, we will capture a scene that millions of people will see on television. When we are finished, we return to camp, unload the precious film, and restock the truck with supplies of film, sound tape, water, and food for the next day.

Do you have any children? Is your family involved in your work?

We do not have children yet; we're too young! This can be a lonely life, but to be truly dedicated to this work, you have to make many sacrifices. The one big one we have made is a normal family life. We cannot live among lions and subject a family to that harsh lifestyle. It would not be fair.

What special preparations do you have to make for your work?

We prepare a lot. If not, we would have died many times over by now. Last New Year's Day our vehicle was stuck in a bog for a day and a half. We were prepared. Our equipment for getting out, like shovels, hi-lift jacks, and winches, was in good working order. We also had enough food and water, sleeping bags and mosquito net, matches, and a cooking pan. Finally, we had a compass so that when we eventually had to give up on getting our vehicle out, we could walk to the nearest village for help. Working alone, we know exactly whose responsibility certain preparations are. Our preparations work like clockwork.

What is the hardest part of your work?

It is not the 127 degrees Fahrenheit heat or the biting tsetse flies; nor is it the odd elephant who stumbles into our tent, trashing our things; or the lions who

Keeping up with lions in Chobe National Park, in Botswana

once stole our solar panel, our only means of talking to the outside world. It may be that at times all this has to end, and we have to make trips to the United States to edit our films. We have to silently say good-bye to the lion cubs we have watched grow up for three years, never knowing if they will be alive when we get back. Editing is stimulating, but the hardest part of the job each time is that one moment on the last day in Africa each time as we look out over our real home of thousands of miles of wilderness...and then drive off to town.

What was your biggest discovery? What are you most proud of?

Scientists always believed that lions and hyenas had a simple, competing relationship. We studied this behavior for five years, then decided to do a film. We worked on the National Geographic film *Eternal Enemies: Lions and Hyenas* for another four years and revealed a relationship that goes beyond normal competition to something more like actual hatred. Today, we are still trying to defend that idea, but it was the first step in trying to open up science to the emotions of animals. Jane Goodall was a pioneer in doing this with chimpanzees. We believe that animals, and elephants in particular, have emotions.

What is left for you to explore?

The possibilities are endless. We are interested in looking beyond the natural history behavior of animals and trying to see and show clear parallels to our own lives and to the meaning of all life. We would love to do a natural history film in space!

Michael Novacek

PALEONTOLOGIST
Birthday: June 3, 1948

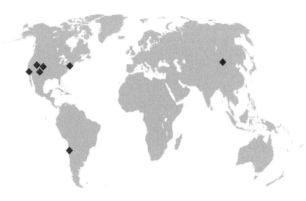

My passion for dinosaurs and other fossils began when I was about seven years old. I had a book called *All About Dinosaurs*, by Roy Chapman Andrews, that was the first of many books that I read and reread on the subject. I was captivated by his account of unearthing dinosaur bones in the Flaming Cliffs of the Gobi, a desert in Mongolia. I vividly remember the drawings of skeletons in the American Museum of Natural History, where I now work, and the etchings of paleontologists lifting huge dinosaur bones on pulleys. My interest wasn't always appreciated by others. When a nun caught me reading about fossils in her class, I was promptly relocated to the section for mystics and dreamers that she called the "spaceman row."

I used to go on explorations with my friends, hunting for whatever small animals we could find in Los Angeles, where I grew up. I've always been able to identify animals. My friends and I could identify different kinds of frogs, lizards, and butterflies. We'd find alligator lizards, which could be very mean and would even bite at us. Even so, we tried, not too successfully, to catch them. Sometimes they would lose their tails, which would then curl and uncurl on the ground for a bit after falling off. Occasionally, I would catch one and take it home and put it in a terrarium. It was fascinating to be able to watch the lizards molt, to actually watch the changes.

My mother had a strong interest in biology and science, and she encouraged my interests, even after I once went hunting dressed in good clothes.

She had specifically warned me to keep clean, but as my friends and I waded into a stagnant pond after a frog, we suddenly found ourselves knee-deep in swamp water. I was a mess.

My family was very supportive of whatever I was into as a child. My father is a jazz musician, and two of my three brothers are professional musicians. One of them is a concert pianist in New York, and the other plays classical guitar in Seattle. My third brother is musical, too, but he has an interesting job designing theme parks for Disney. As I got older, I became more interested in things like music and surfing and socializing. Even though I decided to study biology by the time I went to college at UCLA, I was writing and playing music and not at all certain about becoming a biologist.

One of my teachers at UCLA, Professor Peter Vaughn, invited me to come along one summer on a paleontological expedition. He let me know that I would be the youngest person in the group, and therefore, the work might be beyond me. That, of course, was just the challenge that I needed. I accepted, and over a summer spent in scorching, southern New Mexico, the canyons of Colorado, and the mazes of Utah's Monument Valley, I began to rediscover the passion for exploring that I first felt as a child.

I have, in fact, become a fossil hunter. My passion now lies in exploring how the history of life is revealed by many different kinds of fossils. I can't think of anything more pleasurable and fulfilling than the danger, discomfort, frustration, debate, and criticism that come with this job. It is amazing to me that my work as a paleontologist at the Museum of Natural History in New York City now takes me to the very same Flaming Cliffs that captured my imagination at seven.

Michael J. Novacek

"Make an effort to find out how to follow up on your interests. Tell your friends what you want to do...maybe they are thinking of the same things. Definitely tell your teachers, because they might tell you how to begin to explore what you're interested in."

Michael Novacek

Novacek and Mark Norell remove 600 pounds of sandstone containing bones of an *Oviraptor*.

What was the job that got you started in your field?

The dig that I went on in New Mexico while I was in college gave me my first real experience. I was hooked. Later, because I had gotten something of a reputation for knowing about bones, I was asked to work on a project at the LaBrea Tar Pits, near Los Angeles. I thought, Wow, I can get paid to do this! It was great.

What was the scariest thing that ever happened in your work?

We've been held captive by a renegade army, and we've been shot at. I was once stung by poisonous scorpions. But probably the scariest incident was when my horse fell from underneath me while I was riding in the Andes. My boot caught in the stirrup, and I was dragged behind the horse along the mountain. I was lucky that no bones were broken, but I thought that was really it for me. Because so many things can happen, we try very hard to minimize the danger and take precautions to avoid accidents.

How do you choose a project?

Before each trip we set goals that we hope to accomplish, like mapping an area or collecting a certain type of dinosaur and other fossil bones. We usually can't complete everything. There are always things left to explore from previous visits or new discoveries made on the spot that we will want to follow up on next time.

Sometimes an opportunity just presents itself. The Gobi was known to have a remarkable wealth of fossils, but for more than 60 years Mongolia was closed to Western scientists. In 1990 when the borders were opened, we knew we wanted to go.

Where do you work?

I work in an incredible place—the American Museum of Natural History in New York City—which has more than 32 million specimens and artifacts. People come not only to see them but to continue to do research on them. Some of the dinosaur and mammal fossils that my team and I have found are on display here, including a dinosaur embryo in the egg and a parent *Oviraptor* sitting on a nest of eggs.

A newly discovered therian mammal, only five inches long

My work also takes me to different locations around the world. For several years I have been going on expeditions to the Gobi. The environment can be very harsh, and the heat and isolation can make it difficult at times; but for me there is a lot of beauty to be found in a desert.

What is a normal working day like for you?

When I'm at the museum, I can get a lot of work done in the early morning. I might be in meetings from mid-morning until the afternoon, or I'll look in on some of the many interesting programs going on at the museum. I often go back to my research lab for quiet work in the evening. But there are some evenings for fun with family and friends.

Out in the field the hours can be extremely long because our time there is short, and we want to get as much done as we can. The team might fan out in different directions, so I often spend nine or ten hours straight just walking around alone, looking for stuff. When we find a specimen, we have to remove it from the ground carefully and prepare it to be shipped.

Do you have any children? Is your family involved in your work?

My wife, who is interested in biology, and our daughter, who is in college now, have both come on trips and gotten involved with the work. In fact, my daughter learned how to drive in the Gobi. Since there was nothing for her to hit, she could just get in the car and drive.

What special preparations do you have to make for your work?

As soon as we return from a trip, we start planning for the next one, a year in advance. There is a lot of coordinating to do. In many of the countries I go to, basic supplies are not available. Although I used to travel with just a backpack and a rock hammer like a mountain climber, we now ship over everything from cars to lumber and even the nails we might need. We prepare in advance for transportation, for food and water, for everything.

A lot of preparation goes into removing objects from the ground. When we find a site, we record our location so we can plan to return to the spot in the future. Part of my preparation includes bringing along my lucky bandanna that I've worn in the field for years. I also have a lucky shirt. I'm almost ready to throw it out, by popular demand, but there is talk about at least adding it to the museum memorabilia collections. I think it may have another season, though.

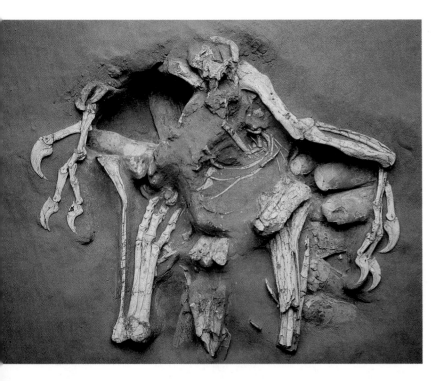

What is the hardest part of your work?

There are hardships like the stinging Gobi sandstorms or rain or having a car get stuck in the mud. But the hardest thing in the field is when things don't go right, when you aren't finding anything of interest. Also, it can be difficult if people on the team aren't getting along or if someone's

Nicknamed "Big Mama," this *Oviraptor* is on view at the American Museum of Natural History.

A sandstorm hits the Gobi.

personality is causing a problem. We've been lucky, because we've had really good people who work together well and share the same passion for what we're doing.

What was your biggest discovery? What are you most proud of?

The discoveries I've made with my research in the lab are as important to me as the discoveries I've made in the field. I am excited about looking at how life has evolved from bacteria to dinosaurs and mammals. Why did one group of creatures survive the Cretaceous extinction event while another didn't? It is in the laboratory that I can investigate the relationship between extinct and living animals.

Red cliffs in the Gobi

My most exciting field discovery occurred in the Gobi. In 1990 my partners, Mark Norell and Malcolm McKenna, and I led the first paleontological expedition to return to the Gobi from the West since Roy Chapman Andrews was there in 1922. Three years later, we decided to head toward the reddish hills we had seen in the distance on our previous visits—an area called Ukhaa Tolgod, which means "small brown hills." When our truck got stuck in mud near the hills, we set up camp. Climbing one of the slopes, we found an incredibly rich site with some dinosaur skeletons scattered right on the surface. It was clear that other scientists had not been there, or the extraordinary specimens would have been collected. As Mark would call out to me that he had found a skull, I'd call back that I'd found one, too. They were all over. We knew that we had come across something special.

What is left for you to explore?

I'm interested in exploring the links between living and extinct species. Birds, for example, are actually examples of living dinosaurs. The modern mammals, including us, diverged from small, unspectacular, shrewlike creatures. How did life evolve on the planet? New technology keeps improving the possibility of new exploration. For instance, satellites are now used to map locations.

I've explored sites on every continent except Australia, but there is always something more that I would like to do.

Check it out:

American Museum of Natural History's
National Center for Science Literacy, Education and Technology

The National Center for Science Literacy, Education and Technology (NCSLET) at The American Museum of Natural History (AMNH) creates programs and materials to connect people of all ages nationwide to the museum's collection of more than 32 million specimens and artifacts. More than 200 research scientists associated with AMNH participate in an interactive Web site. It's designed to let you do such things as join in an exploration of the Gobi as scientists unearth dinosaur fossils. You can help build a rain forest or take off for Mars and learn virtually firsthand about our neighboring planet.

You might be interested in trying for one of the new Young Naturalist Awards that honor students in grades 7 through 12 for excellence in biology, earth science, and astronomy.

Velociraptor skull

Find out more:
The National Center for Science Literacy, Education and Technology at the American Museum of Natural History. Phone: (212) 769-5993; Online: www.amnhonline.org/nationalcenter/

Johan Reinhard

ANTHROPOLOGIST
Birthday: December 13, 1943

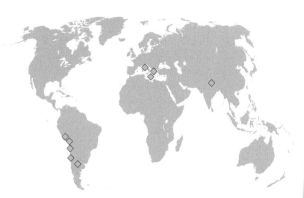

veryone seems surprised when I tell them that I grew up in a small town in the Midwest. I have lived most of my life outside the United States, and even my name is foreign. But the truth is I was born and lived the first 18 years of my life in New Lenox, a village of 800 people in Illinois farm country.

My early adventures were hunting, fishing, and camping along Hickory Creek, which flowed through our town. Like many of my friends, I collected fossils and arrowheads, read *The Hardy Boys*, and experimented with rockets, most of which exploded on the launch pad. Unlike my friends, I began to read more about explorers and was soon dreaming of visiting faraway lands. One book in particular, *The Book of Marvels*, got me interested in exploration and in thinking that I could do what the author did when he was still a boy.

At 16, my first chance to be on my own came when I joined a railroad line gang of men from the South working throughout the Midwest. Digging holes by hand, we put up telegraph poles. The men were much older than I and came from much different backgrounds. They seemed like people from another world, and in a way they were. As a young Northerner, I had to act and talk like them to be accepted. Unknowingly, I was behaving like an anthropologist, always learning about how these strange men thought. Maybe more important, I found I could do hard labor and earn my own keep—and thus my independence.

When I graduated from high school, I traveled alone to South America with money saved from working on the line gang. It was during that trip that I knew

I was fascinated by other cultures. I decided that I wanted to learn more about civilizations of the past and about people living totally different lives from mine in other parts of the world. I could not believe my luck when I found there was an actual profession for this type of work—anthropology.

The more I read about anthropology, the more I thought that I should learn various tools to use in different locations or situations in the future. Some of these tools were academic ones like linguistics, which taught me how to learn languages still unknown and unwritten. Others were less academic and included skydiving, scuba diving, mountain climbing, cave exploring, and sailing. I thought that these skills would enable me to undertake exploration in places that few, if any, anthropologists had worked before.

After studying anthropology for a couple of years in the United States, it seemed only logical that, if I was going to be an anthropologist and live in other cultures and speak other languages, I might as well study anthropology in a foreign country and kill two birds with one stone! So I went to Europe, studied German, and then continued my studies at the University of Vienna, in Austria.

My first cultural anthropological field experience with sponge divers in Greece was soon followed by my first archaeological experience underwater in the Mediterranean. But my main desire was to gain experience in a culture as different from my own as possible, so I focused on studying nomadic hunter-gatherers. Only a few such societies existed in the world, and one was in the foothills of the Himalaya. I was interested in how they maintained their way of life and what happened when some groups of their tribe settled down and took up agriculture. Above all, I was fascinated by their religion.

My interests in mountains, religion, and archaeology all grew together until I found that they merged in a unique way in the Andes. There, mountain worship led people to build the world's highest known archaeological sites, and my research over a 16-year period eventually led to the discovery of the Inca Ice Maiden.

What was the job that got you started in your field?

Ironically, my first job in archaeology was also one of the most interesting that I have ever had. I was 21 years old and studying anthropology at the University of Vienna, in Austria, when I got to work with one of the fathers of underwater archaeology, Peter Throckmorton. We spent the summer of 1965 conducting underwater archaeological surveys in the Mediterranean and in a lake in Italy.

First, we recovered Roman artifacts off the coast of southern Italy. Then, in the north we surveyed a village site of the 3,000-year-old Villanovan culture, 16 feet below Lake Bolsena. We uncovered never-before-seen artifacts. Not only did I learn how to do archaeology in the field (even if underwater!), but I participated in some of the most exciting research being done at the time.

At work in Lake Titicaca, in Bolivia

"Most people think you need physical strength and scientific intelligence, but one of the most overlooked things anthropologists and explorers need is the desire to understand and respect people who think differently than they do. Patience, hard work, and a good sense of humor are indispensable and may be enough for you to be an asset to many expeditions."

Johan Reinhard

What was the scariest thing that ever happened in your work?

I have had many close calls while working or training for work, especially while in the mountains. But the scariest was the one that lasted the longest. I was 20 years old and climbing alone (very foolishly) on a mountain in Europe, when I started falling down a snow-covered slope. I frantically used my ice ax to slow myself by putting my weight on its point while holding it against my chest. I could hardly believe my luck when I gradually stopped. But to my horror, I soon found myself falling again, and only then did I realize that I actually was on top

Reinhard tackles a crevasse on Cerro Morado, in Chile.

of a slab of falling ice! I was being swept off the mountainside toward a drop of more than 2,000 feet and certain death. There was nothing I could do.

After what seemed like several minutes—but must have been only seconds—the slab came to a stop. This time I knew that if I moved it might start sliding again. I waited awhile, then slowly, very slowly, made my way sideways to a stable area. I was still so frightened that I continued down using both hands and feet, although the descent was easy the rest of the way.

Working on mountain summits is occasionally dangerous, more due to weather than difficulties in climbing. Electrical storms are especially to be feared, and even a twisted ankle can cause serious problems at heights of more than 20,000 feet. But I view this as part of the job and not much more dangerous than walking city streets at night or driving in rush-hour traffic. Accidents can mostly be avoided if you are physically and mentally prepared and carefully plan your work.

How do you choose a project?

I choose a project after weighing several factors: Will it potentially provide new knowledge or be beneficial to people? Will I learn from it, both in a scientific sense and in terms of my own personal growth? Can I do the job as well as, or better, than others who might do it? Will I regret not having done it even if it is unsuccessful? If I can answer yes to those questions, then the rest is easy.

The Inca Trail leads to Machu Picchu.

Where do you work?

These days I am mostly in mountain environments, either in the Himalaya or the Andes. Usually, various forms of transportation take me to work: first, a plane to reach the country or city; then a vehicle to get nearer to the mountain; then sometimes a mule or horse to get to the foot of the mountain; and finally, a trek or a climb to the archaeological sites higher on a mountain. I have worked in deserts and jungles before, but I much prefer the mountains.

What is a normal working day like for you?

At a mountain site, I usually have a simple breakfast while waiting for the sun to rise and warm up (a little, anyway!) our campsite. I check my gear, the weather, and my teammates to see that all is well. We go over the work plan, then climb to the actual site to begin surveying and excavating ruins. At the end of the day, we make sure our finds are well protected and our notes are up to date, then return to camp to discuss the next day's program, write up any further notes...and have a very welcome hot meal.

   In the city, my day consists of writing, reading, answering correspondence—in short, the normal hard work that turns discoveries and information obtained on the mountain into data others can use.

Do you have any children? Is your family involved in your work?

I have never had children—my way of life would be mentally and physically hard for them. In the field, I thought they might lack good schooling; and left behind, they would grow up without a father around much. I also did not think I could earn enough money to live such a life and also raise a family.

Unlike even many other anthropologists, I prefer to spend long periods in the field. I lived most of the last 28 years outside the United States, and once I did not set foot in the United States for 9 years solid! But I have been in the field with close companions who have shared in the work in some way.

What special preparations do you have to make for your work?

My work involves using not only the usual tools of archaeology (such as measuring tapes, notebooks, cameras, trowels, brushes, etc.), but also mountaineering equipment (like ice axes, backpacks, ropes, altimeters, climbing boots, and special sleeping bags, clothing, stoves, and tents) and medical supplies for emergencies. I keep a checklist with categories for each kind of equipment I need.

By necessity, I was often alone when I began years ago, but now I work with others. With a team of about six people, the minimum necessary to do a high-altitude excavation well, a couple of people can work while the others rest.

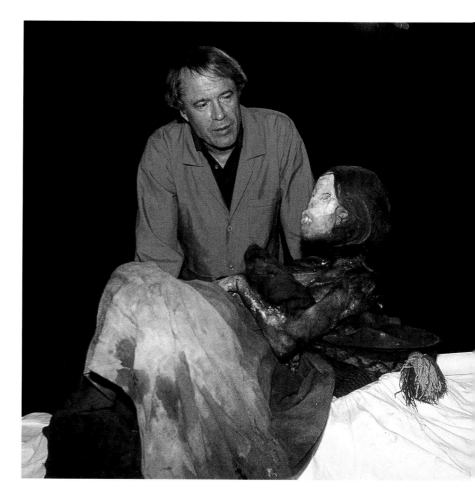

Reinhard with the Inca Ice Maiden, discovered when her 500-year-old tomb broke apart in the Andes

What is the hardest part of your work?

The hardest thing is to keep a team working hard over several days when everyone suffers some effects of the altitude. We usually work above 17,000 feet, and often much higher. People tire quickly, lose their appetites, do not sleep well, and often feel ill with headaches, nausea, coughs, sore throats, and colds.

Amid ice formations in Argentina

In the city the hardest thing is keeping up with all of the reports, project proposals, people who want something from me or whom I must contact for information, and reading new scientific publications that relate to the project.

What was your biggest discovery? What are you most proud of?

The biggest discovery I ever made was probably the frozen Inca mummy—the Ice Maiden—that I located at 20,700 feet. It is one of the best preserved mummies from ancient times, and it has provided a wealth of information.

I am most proud, however, of the totality of my work relating to mountain worship and high-altitude archaeology. This is because it has led both to new discoveries, like the Ice Maiden and many other rare artifacts, and to an increased understanding of Andean cultures. I have developed better explanations for some of archaeology's greatest mysteries, like the giant drawings in the desert in Peru and the ruins of Machu Picchu. Discoveries I have made in my mind have been more exciting to me than those I have made in the field.

What is left for you to explore?

I could never undertake all of the projects on my list, even if I were a billionaire. I hope to do more high-altitude excavations in the Andes. Few scientific excavations have been done there, and they yield unique, well-preserved artifacts and a wealth of information about Inca religion. At the top of my list, so to speak, is the world's highest known archaeological site at 22,000 feet, which I have surveyed twice but never excavated.

Check it out:
The Mountain Institute

The Mountain Institute (TMI) brings over 25 years of experience to community-based conservation of natural and cultural resources, environmental education, and outdoor adventure. Working in some of the oldest, longest, and highest mountain ranges in the world—the Appalachians, the Andes, and the Himalaya—TMI's learning-by-doing approach provides geology lessons atop a summit or within a cave, along a mountain waterway, or in an old-growth hemlock grove. Learn the specific skills needed for backcountry travel and exploration: rock climbing, canoeing, backpacking, orienteering, kayaking, and caving. Every distant mountaintop is a new adventure.

Dr. Johan Reinhard is a senior research fellow at the Mountain Institute. In 1997 he set up a portable communications office on a Peruvian mountaintop and transmitted firsthand information about his expedition via his Web site. Using advanced technology and rugged equipment, Dr. Reinhard was able to communicate with the rest of the world, even under the harsh conditions of an extremely high altitude. A sophisticated satellite phone links the mountaintop office to anywhere in the world, and a digital camera and camcorder transmit photographs and videos.

The National Geographic Society, which helped sponsor Dr. Reinhard during the many years of exploration that led to the discovery of the Inca Ice Maiden, maintains information about the Inca Ice Maiden and about Dr. Reinhard's ongoing work on its Web site.

Find out more:
Dr. Johan Reinhard: www.reinhard.sympatico.ca
The Mountain Institute: www.mountain.org
The National Geographic Society:
www.nationalgeographic.com

Rick C. West

ARACHNOLOGIST
Birthday: December 3, 1951

I was born in the city of Victoria on Vancouver Island, British Columbia, in Canada. Before I began school, I lived in the country with my parents and my younger brother and sister. I had no friends my age nearby, and older children teased me because of my bad stutter. My brother and sister were too young to play with, so I spent most of my time wandering in nearby meadows or along the ocean tidal pools.

I enjoyed collecting frogs, snakes, insects, and crabs, and sometimes I'd bring them home. My parents made me release them, explaining that they should always be left in the wild, because they would die as pets. I was allowed, though, to collect and raise caterpillars. My mother would take me to the city to talk with the late Dr. Clifford Carl of the Royal British Columbia Museum about the habits of the creatures I brought to show him.

In elementary school my stuttering grew worse, as did the teasing, and as a result I was a poor student. To encourage me to read and improve my grades, the principal let me choose books to read to him several times a week. I always chose insect and reptile books. In fifth grade my family moved to the city, and I met other children who shared my interest in insects and animals. My stuttering improved, and the teasing gradually stopped by junior high, when my best subject was biology and my worst was mathematics.

My interest in tarantulas began in my early teens during summer visits to relatives in Poway, in San Diego County, California. My cousin Victor showed me local reptiles and insects in the hills there. One day in a citrus orchard, I spotted holes in the ground with white silk over them. When I asked what they were, I was told, "Tarantulas live in there!" I couldn't believe that something I'd only seen in horror movies or read about in scary books could be living in holes in the ground in my cousin's backyard...and he wasn't afraid.

I got a shovel and dug into the hole. All of a sudden, the dirt moved and out scrambled a huge brown tarantula. At first, it appeared to me to be as big as a guinea pig. I caught the hairy beast in a carton and was totally mesmerized by it, looking at it every hour over the next few days. When it came time to go home, I couldn't let it go. With my aunt's and uncle's assurances that tarantulas were harmless, and mine that I would be careful, my parents let me bring it back to Victoria. I remember I wanted to hold it but couldn't find any information on how bad its bite was or if tarantulas were truly dangerous or aggressive. It sounds silly now, but for the first few months I wore leather gloves to hold the spider. Gradually, seeing that it wasn't going to bite, I began handling it with my bare hands. I found great satisfaction in being able to dispel the unfounded fear of tarantulas.

During my college years I was encouraged by my biology professor, Mrs. Ruby Littlepage, and my entomology professor, Dr. Richard Ring, to continue with arachnology. Later I was made an honorary research associate at the local museum, specializing in the field of arachnology, but there were no jobs in Victoria for arachnologists. I went to work for the local Society for the Prevention of Cruelty to Animals and have been employed with them for 23 years, now as Chief Special Constable. It was here I met and married the woman I love, Lynn West.

My study of tarantulas has taken me to the southwestern United States, Kenya, Tanzania, Mexico, Nicaragua, Costa Rica, Panama, Colombia, Venezuela, Brazil, Peru, and to Trinidad and Tobago. I now assist other scientific institutions, scientists, and hobbyists around the world with questions or with identifying tarantula spiders.

Rick C. West

"No matter what anyone says to you, don't give up or be discouraged from pursuing your dream."

Rick C. West

West holding a giant tarantula in a Piaroa Indian community in Amazonas, in southern Venezuela.

What was the job that got you started in your field?

In the mid-1970s I joined the newly formed American Tarantula Society, which is still active today. The society is made up of hobbyists and a few researchers and scientists who have the same fascination for tarantulas as I do. Their goal is to promote the study of these spiders and share information about them to dispel their bad reputation. I wrote and shared many articles in their monthly journal and, in return, learned more about tarantulas from reading others' stories. If you know a lot about something, be it stamps, tropical fish, reptiles, or any subject, find a club or society and share that information with others.

What was the scariest thing that ever happened in your work?

My work can be dangerous when I am in a rain forest or a country where I don't know anyone. I've walked into quicksand in Panama while working alone and had a hard time getting free. I was stung by a scorpion while alone in the bush in Mexico and had to get immediate help because I had trouble breathing. In southern Venezuela my partner and I watched Yanomami Indian men dance and take hallucinogenic drugs until an interpreter explained that they had just attacked and killed several other Indian men in a neighboring village and were preparing for a counterattack. We quickly left!

Now I always hire a guide who knows the people and dangers to avoid in an area. And I also have to watch out for poisonous snakes. I consider my work both exciting and dangerous but wouldn't change it for anything.

How do you choose a project?

I choose tarantula projects that will give me the best opportunity to study and photograph new species as well as other fauna and flora I've not seen before. I can only get away on a project when I'm not needed as much at my main job. Also, money always controls where I go and how long I will be away. As I love my wife very much, I try not to be away much longer than three weeks at a time.

Where do you work?

I work primarily in both deserts and rain forests. I take a plane to get to the closest city or town, then organize a guide and jeep to get into the very remote and unpopulated regions. In the Amazon, where roads are scarce or impassable, I take a small riverboat or dugout canoe to get deeper into the rain forest. I've used helicopters to reach the tops of mountains in Venezuela to study tarantulas. I won't go into a country having a civil war or involved in drug trafficking.

What is a normal working day like for you?

Tarantulas are mainly active at night, so I do most of my study and photography at night. By day I look for good areas to search by night, or I photograph other animals and plants. Usually, I get out of the hammock at 6 a.m., eat a good camp breakfast, and head into the desert or forest. By noon it's too hot to work, so I return to camp to write notes, organize and clean equipment, or study and photograph the tarantulas that have been caught. Due to the heat, I often skip lunch and just have an early dinner so I can get into the forest or desert just as the tarantulas are emerging from their burrows. Sometimes I don't go to bed until about 1 a.m.

West (right), Dr. Mark Moffat (left), and guide Juan Carlos Ramirez capture a tarantula.

A helicopter takes West to hunt rare tarantulas in a mountaintop rain forest.

Do you have any children? Is your family involved in your work?

I have three grown children, two boys and a girl. None of them has an interest in tarantulas. My family is very proud of my work. My wife, Lynn, is strongly supportive and often gives me the encouragement and drive not to give up. When I first met Lynn, though, she had an inexplicable fear of all spiders. Now, with our basement full of live and preserved tarantulas, she no longer fears them. In fact, she feeds and cares for more than 600 live tarantulas when I'm away on trips. One of the "house rules," however, is that I can't let any of the tarantulas escape into the house from their enclosed room. Otherwise, Lynn has threatened to finish them off with two cans of insecticide!

What special preparations do you have to make for your work?

Going into remote areas to study tarantulas, I take camera equipment, flashlights, lanterns, lots of batteries, insect repellent, a medical kit, a hammock, anti-malaria netting and tablets, a snakebite kit, machete, knives, a small shovel, a backpack, high leather boots, collecting equipment, preserving alcohol, maps, local animal and plant identification books, and lots of clothes I can get dirty.

I always wear my bowie knife as good luck. When my children were younger, I would tease them and say, "Give me a bowie knife, and I can live anywhere!" I never travel alone anymore for safety reasons. I always make a checklist before leaving on a trip, but I usually forget something.

What is the hardest part of your work?

The hardest part about being away while studying tarantulas is the loneliness and wishing I could share some beautiful moments with my wife. You forget how harsh field conditions can be until you're actually back in the field again— then you may find you wish you were back home in comfort.

The second hardest thing is the difficulty in bringing live or dead tarantulas home for scientific study. In countries where tarantulas live, most people kill them on sight. Their governments make it nearly impossible to take tarantulas out of these countries to study in order to educate people about this misunderstood creature. I am also very sad at times to see the large destruction of rain forests or deserts by humans before researchers are able to learn about the plants and animals that live in them and how they might be important to us.

West shares a cooked tarantula with a Piaroa chief in Amazonas.

What was your biggest discovery? What are you most proud of?

I am most proud of initiating the story for and being the scientific adviser on the film *Giant Tarantula*. This film not only shows the natural history of giant tarantulas in the rain forest, but also shows how the Piaroa Indians of southern Venezuela use these giant spiders as a valuable food source and in their spiritual ceremonies. It is important to have an appreciation and respect for other cultures.

Tarantulas have been misunderstood, and I think this is partly because of the way they were depicted in horror books and movies in the past. Tarantulas were once thought to be deadly poisonous. However, I do not know of a single human fatality directly related to the effects of their poison. Some people are also afraid of spiders in general, and tarantulas especially, because they are the largest and hairiest of spiders. I am proud of the fact that nature documentaries have helped to correct some of the harmful stories about tarantulas.

What is left for you to explore?

I will always look to explore regions beyond where other researchers have been. I will always want to look for and study those yet undiscovered tarantulas. I am now working on a tarantula film for Discovery Television-Canada and have tarantula study trips planned for Peru and possibly East Africa. I don't know what lies ahead for me—I just appreciate my good health, the love and support of my family, and every day as it comes.

Juris Zarins

ARCHAEOLOGIST
Birthday: February 17, 1945

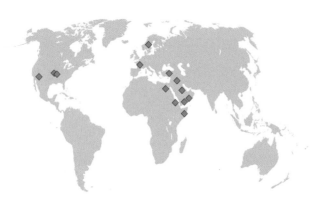

My family emigrated from Latvia to the United States via Germany in the early 1950s. When I was in fifth grade, my teacher nominated me to attend a lab school at the University of Nebraska in Lincoln. So from seventh grade through high school I benefited from small classes and a university atmosphere. My high school biology teacher told me that the Smithsonian Institution was looking for students to conduct archaeological work as "shovel bums," so I applied and was accepted. I'd never heard of the Smithsonian, but I needed a summer job.

The first year conducting river basin surveys for the Smithsonian was a real eye-opener. As a young student I was thrown together with archaeologists and college kids from all over the United States to excavate sites in the Oahe Dam Reservoir, in South Dakota. My eyes were opened to a world of vast South Dakota spaces, searing heat, poverty-stricken Brule Sioux Indians, and the fascinating archaeology of the fort system of Lewis and Clark.

Before that summer I had never considered an outdoor job that would involve working unusual hours, meeting all sorts of people, and camping out. The following summer, when I got to work for the Smithsonian again, I decided that this was what I wanted to do as a career. My parents thought my interest was strange and wanted me to become a doctor or lawyer. Nevertheless, they agreed to help me pursue my interest in archaeology.

I was captivated by archaeology because it opened a world of exotica. It

82 ◆◆◆ Talking with Adventurers

helped solve riddles of the past and brought a better understanding to the present. My mother had instilled in me a love of learning, particularly history, geography, and languages. I saw archaeology as a way to combine adventure, outdoor living, and meeting people. So in school, I really concentrated on history. As a senior in high school, I took my first anthropology course with Dr. Edward Fry at the University of Nebraska. When I later entered the University of Nebraska as a freshman, I had made up my mind to be an archaeologist, so I took archaeology, anthropology, and a lot of geology courses.

As a child I had often gone to the University of Nebraska museum to see fossil mammoths, mastodons, saber-tooths, hippos, camels, and horses. These animals all roamed Nebraska up to thousands of years ago. The museum was a treasure mine of vertebrate fossils collected from western Nebraska, or the Badlands as it is called. I guess my love for archaeology had already been stimulated by my early love for geology. To this day, I send students with geology backgrounds to also study archaeology. They learn remote sensing, space imagery, and surveying as well.

I now teach gifted junior high school students, ages 10 to 13, at Drury College in Springfield, Missouri, in a program called Summerscape. We are able to interest students in archaeology earlier than when I went to school. Just last year in Parsons, Kansas, we had a training dig for second graders. Fifty second graders are hard to beat! Students often get excited about archaeology through the classroom, fieldwork, or through computers.

Archaeology requires so much interest in everything people did: what foods they ate; plants they grew; tools they used; and what their houses, clothing, and jewelry looked like. Archaeologists need many tools to understand the past, so a variety of fields of study are useful. Botany, geology, and photography might not seem related, but they are very important, for example, in analyzing the tools people used or types of clothes they wore.

Nothing is ever boring about archaeology.

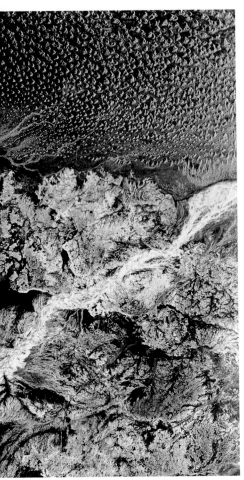
NASA satellite image of Shisur Ubar

What was the job that got you started in your field?

In addition to the fieldwork I did for the river basin surveys with the Smithsonian Institution, I also worked when I was a student for the Field Museum of Chicago on a site in northern Arizona. As a college senior I worked on Upper Paleolithic material in France and on an Iron Age site in Sweden. When I went to graduate school, I had a job in eastern Turkey on the Keban Dam Project and at Nippur, in Iraq.

My first professional job was doing desert archaeology in Saudi Arabia in 1975. I worked for the Ministry of Education while living in Riyadh full time with my wife and child. That was quite an experience! Archaeology had never been done in Saudi Arabia before this, and no foreigners had ever lived in Riyadh. It was very exciting because we found all sorts of fantastic sites. After ten years of working there, I developed a real sense of how to look for sites in the desert.

What was the scariest thing that ever happened in your work?

Dangerous is certainly a term we could use in desert work. Going into the desert without adequate preparation and sufficient supplies is very dangerous. Breaking down in the desert with little water could mean death.

Getting lost is another real concern. In the great Empty Quarter, a desert region in the southeastern interior of the Arabian Peninsula, the dunes are 600 feet high, and it is easy to lose one's way without navigational equipment. We also have to watch out for vipers—very dangerous snakes—when we are at a site. Putting your hands in dark places where snakes and scorpions can attack is really scary! Mostly, though, I consider work in the desert to be adventurous, because we discover remote, abandoned sites that have sometimes been unseen for hundreds of thousands of years.

How do you choose a project?

I answer three questions: First, will we receive permission to work on a site from the government of a country? Second, can we obtain the financial support for the project? And last, will we be able to interest others in helping us?

"Archaeology is for kids who are different, see the world differently, have great imaginations, and want to see how people lived in the past. America is a great place to find your opportunity, since there are so many schools specializing in some region of the world, some special group of people, or some interesting period."

Juris Zarins

Making notes at the Lost City of Ubar

I started off working in Arabia, a peninsula surrounded by all sorts of interesting places like the Red Sea, Mesopotamia, and Iran and interesting people like the Sumerians, Egyptians, nomads, and Yemenis. Being there led me to many other places and people that have become the focus for other projects.

Where do you work?

I always find myself in desert areas, but they can look very different. Some are rocky or hilly or have large areas of dunes. Some desert areas are coastal or near ancient springs. We get to a site by four-wheel-drive vehicles and then we walk, walk, walk. You cannot see anything if you do not walk. I generally avoid going to huge dune areas by myself, and I make sure that we have several vehicles and plenty of gas and water.

What is a normal working day like for you?

A normal working day consists of getting up early, getting all the gear together, readying the cars, and checking equipment. Sometimes we drive a long way, forget something essential, like water, and have to go back. We eat a pack lunch in the field and then work until 4 or 5 p.m. In the Middle East, we primarily work during the winter. After supper we wash, look at artifacts, write about our work that day, then take a break and go to bed early. Usually, we have little or no artificial light to work by, so we have to work during the day.

Do you have any children? Is your family involved in your work?

My wife is an organist and works in a program that helps teenage moms. We have five children, who are all teenagers or older now. My whole family worked on the Shisur Ubar site, where the Lost City of Ubar is located, when my children were younger. In fact, when my oldest son was three and a half, he was probably the first foreign child in the Nefud Desert.

They all worked with me again in the field during the summer of 1995, and, of course, I made them excavate. Usually, they do not want to go to the field with me once they find out how much work it is. However, one of my daughters, Ingrid, still loves fieldwork. She has done underwater archaeology and worked in Oman with me.

What special preparations do you have to make for your work?

Generally I take basic clothes and a dig kit consisting of trowels, picks, string, notebooks, and tapes for measuring. I always take a hat. Most of the other equipment and supplies, especially food, I find in the towns of the Middle East where we are working. Sometimes I bring peanut butter, which cannot be found locally.

Archaeologists can work alone, but it is better to work in a group. Students often work with us. With their help, we can find more sites, move more dirt out of the way, map a site more quickly, take more photographs, and carry more equipment and other things. Experts such as geologists, botanists, and zoologists also come along on an expedition for part of the time.

Zarins and team excavate the south wall and the tower at Shisur Ubar, in Oman.

What is the hardest part of your work?

The hardest part of my work is being lonely. The days are long, and I miss my family, teaching school, and my friends. I am a sports nut. I like to play basketball and tennis and watch all sorts of sports on television, so I miss that very much when I am in the field.

What was your biggest discovery? What are you most proud of?

Our biggest discovery was the Shisur Ubar find in Oman. We felt really good about that find, because it cast light on Near Eastern history and Matthew's biblical account of the Wise Men bringing myrrh to the Christ Child. The fragrances frankincense and myrrh come from only two places in the southern part of the Arabian Peninsula, and one of them is Shisur Ubar.

I am also really proud of our work in the Eastern Desert in Egypt. We found evidence that the pharaohs had authorized expeditions to the area around the Red Sea to look for frankincense and myrrh as long ago as 3000 B.C. We actually found artifacts from their encampments.

What is left for you to explore?

For the future, we are moving into Yemen, the area where myrrh comes from. Then we will move into northern Somalia, working together with Dr. Steve Brandt of the University of Florida, and into Eritrea to learn about the African side of the Red Sea.

Nicholas Clapp, Andy Dunsire, and Ron Blom, part of Zarins's expedition team, consult on a GPS fix in the Wadi Mitan, in the Sultanate of Oman.

Check it out:

Summerscape

Summerscape, a summer program for gifted children currently enrolled in grades six through nine, is held at Drury College in Springfield, Missouri. Students from all over the United States and around the world are offered an opportunity to enhance their areas of interest, investigate new ideas, and interact with their peers in a caring, safe, and fun learning environment.

A small sampling of Summerscape courses includes: Right Brain Drawing, Computers in Design, Bug Off!, and Speleology: Underground Adventure! Dr. Juris Zarins teaches an archaeology course that explores where ancient people lived and how archaeologists work. Field trips take students to actual archaeological sites, and lab work encourages understanding of archaeological tools and methods.

The ruins of ancient Shisur Ubar, also known as the Lost City of Ubar.

Find out more:
Summerscape
Drury College, Belle Hall 206
900 N. Benton Avenue
Springfield, MO 65802
Phone: 417-873-7386

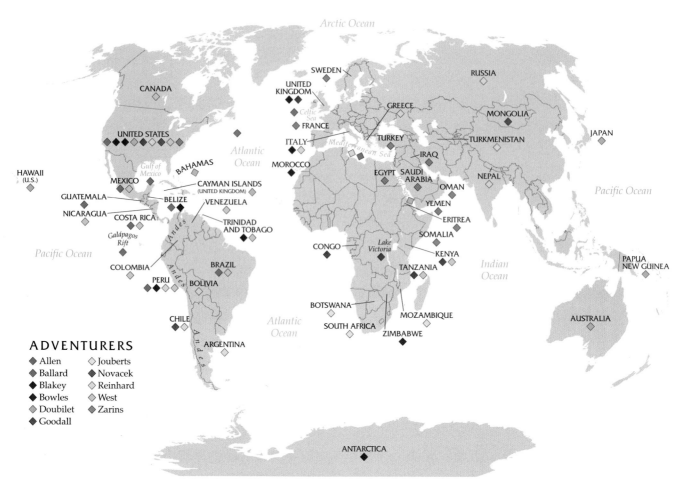

ADVENTURERS

- ◆ Allen
- ◇ Jouberts
- ◆ Ballard
- ◆ Novacek
- ◆ Blakey
- ◇ Reinhard
- ◆ Bowles
- ◇ West
- ◇ Doubilet
- ◆ Zarins
- ◆ Goodall

Diamonds color coded to each adventurer show the general locations
of fieldwork sites mentioned in this book.

Glossary

ANTHROPOLOGIST ....A scientist who studies the origin, behavior, physical, social, and cultural development of human beings.

ALTIMETER ....An instrument for determining elevation.

ANTIVENIN ....A remedy to counter or neutralize the effects of poison from an animal such as a snake, spider, or scorpion.

ARACHNOLOGIST ....A scientist who studies spiders.

ARCHAEOLOGIST ....A scientist who recovers and studies the material evidence left from past human life and culture.

BIOACOUSTICIAN ....A scientist who studies animal communication and animal sound perception.

BENDS ....Pains in the joints and abdomen that occur when a diver rises too quickly from a great depth to the surface of the ocean. The pain is a result of nitrogen bubbles that form in the blood and tissues.

CETACEAN ....Any of the many aquatic mammals of the order Cetacea, which includes whales, dolphins, and porpoises. These mammals are characterized by nearly hairless bodies, broad flippers, and flat, notched tails.

CHICLE POT ....A pot made from the wood of the sapodilla tree found in Mexico and Central America.

CIRCADIAN RHYTHM ....A daily rhythmic activity cycle, based on 24-hour intervals that is exhibited by many living organisms.

DUGONG ....A plant-eating marine mammal that lives in the tropical coastal waters of the Indian Ocean, Red Sea, and southwest Pacific Ocean. It has flippers for forelimbs and a deeply notched tail fin. It is related to the manatee.

EMBOLISM ....A dangerous blockage of a blood vessel usually caused by an air bubble.

EMU ....A large, flightless Australian bird related to and resembling an ostrich.

EPIGRAPHER ....A person who studies and decodes ancient inscriptions.

EXOTICA ....Things that are curiously unusual or excitingly strange.

ETHOLOGIST ....A scientist who studies animal behavior, especially under natural conditions.

EXPLORER ....A person who searches or travels an area for the purpose of discovery.

FOSSIL ....A remnant or trace of something that lived in a past geologic age, such as a skeleton or a leaf imprint embedded and preserved in the earth's crust.

GEOPHYSICS .... A branch of earth science dealing with the physical processes and phenomena occurring especially in the earth and in its vicinity.

GPS .... The global positioning systems technology, which receives longitude and latitude coordinates from satellites in order to map the location of a remote site.

HYDROTHERMAL .... Of or relating to hot water.

HYENA .... Any of several meat-eating mammals of the family Hyaenidae that live in Africa and Asia. It has short hind legs, coarse hair, and powerful jaws.

ICHTHYOLOGIST .... A scientist who specializes in the branch of zoology that deals with the study of fishes.

JUNGLE .... An area of land that is densely overgrown with tropcal vegetation. Often used as another word for rain forest.

LEATHERBACK .... The largest living sea turtle. It is found in tropical waters and gets its name from its tough, leathery shell.

MAMMALOGIST .... A scientist who studies any of the warm-blooded, vertebrates of the class Mammalia, which includes human beings.

MANTA RAY .... Also called a devilfish or sea devil, this fish lives in tropical and subtropical seas. It has a large flattened body, winglike pectoral fins, a whiplike tail, and two hornlike fins projecting forward from its head. The word "manta" is Spanish for "blanket," which is what the fish resembles.

MORPHO .... Any of various large, brightly colored butterflies of the genus *Morpho* that are found in tropical parts of Central and South America. They are known for the brilliant blue color of their wings.

MYRRH .... An aromatic gum resin that comes from certain trees and shrubs in the southern Arabian Peninsula and eastern Africa. Also called balm of Gilead, it is used in making perfume and incense.

NEUROPHYSIOLOGIST .... A scientist who studies the function of the nervous system in living organisms.

NOMADS .... People who have no fixed home and who move from place to place according to the seasons, searching for food, water, and grazing land.

OVIRAPTOR .... A dinosaur that got its name in 1923, possibly unfairly, when a skull was found lying over a nest of dinosaur eggs. The name comes from "ovi", meaning "egg," and "raptor," meaning "robber." In fact, it may have been protecting the nest.

PALEONTOLOGIST .... A scientist who studies the fossils of plants and animals from prehistoric or past geologic periods.

PINNIPED .... One of a group of carnivorous amphibious mammals, including seals, walruses, and sea lions that have paddle-like limbs.

PIT VIPER .... A poisonous snake that gets its name from the heat-sensing pits located behind its nostrils. Hunting mostly by night, the viper uses this sensory organ to detect slight differences in temperature given off by the bodies of its warm-blooded prey. In a sudden strike, the pit viper uses its single pair of long, hollow fangs to inject a poisonous combination of neuro (nerve) and hemo (blood) toxins into its victim. Rattlenakes and copperheads—and the fer-de-lance—are pit vipers.

POACHER .... A person who hunts animals illegally.

RAIN FOREST .... A dense, broadleaf evergreen forest that has an annual rainfall of at least 200 centimeters (80 inches). Most rain forests are in tropical regions.

RAIN FOREST ECOLOGIST .... A scientist who studies the relationship between rain forest plants and animals.

REMOTE SENSING .... Obtaining information about an area or object without touching it. For instance, remote sensing technology allows archaeologists to "see" an archaeological site either from the air or the ground without actual excavation. On land a radar device is dragged over a site, giving a rough picture of any structure underneath. From the air satellites read visible light as well as the infrared bands of the electromagnetic spectrum and use radar signals to penetrate the earth's surface.

RHEA...A flightless South American bird that resembles a small ostrich but that has three toes instead of two.

SKUA ....A large, predatory sea bird.

TELEPRESENCE..........................The "you are there" feeling conveyed by real-time video transmission of images and sounds.

THERIAN ....A member of the subclass of mammals that includes the modern placental and marsupial mammals.

TUBE WORMS.............................Any of the annelids, or worms and wormlike creatures, that live in the tubular cases that they secrete or glue together from grit.

UNDERWATER PHOTOGRAPHER..A person who takes pictures under water using special camera equipment.

VELOCIRAPTOR ....An agile and very speedy killer dinosaur from the Cretaceous geologic period, during which dinosaurs died out.

WILDLIFE FILMMAKER ....A person who makes movies about animals, etc. in their natural environments.

YAGI ANTENNA..........................A directional antenna (named for its inventor) used to localize the signal from an animal's radio transmitter.

Acknowledgments & Photo Credits

From our first phone call to our last photocopy, many people helped us assemble the information and pictures for this book. We especially want to thank our editor, Barbara Lalicki, for her vision, her insights, and her constant support. Thanks also to Jennifer Emmett for her hard work and good humor; to Faythe Weaver, Web Sherpa; and to all of the following who helped to smooth the path: Luisa Avila, Kristin Begle, Dr. Ron Blom, Dan Buettner, Dr. Allan F. Burns, Nicholas Clapp, Kelly Coladarci, Anne Doubilet, Maria Gallagher, Emily Goldberg, Mona Jasnow, Jennifer Lindsey, Dr. Hassan Minor, Kalila Minor, Cathy Offinger, LeeAnn Shreve, Barbara Werscheck, and Annette White.

Grateful acknowledgment is given to the adventurers who, despite their arduous schedules, contributed their time, shared their experiences, and assembled photos and other materials for this book. We would also like to thank the organizations and individuals listed by chapter below:

ALLEN: 8 Jack Allen; 12 and 14 Dan Buettner; 13 Doug Mason/MayaQuest; 15 (bottom) Doug Mason/MayaQuest; back cover Nicole Gottdenker. All other photographs courtesy of Christina M. Allen.

BALLARD: 16 Harriet Ballard; 18 (top) and 20 (left) Jonathan S. Blair; 18 (bottom) courtesy of Woods Hole Oceanographic Institution; 19 and 20 (right) Emory Kristof; 21 Joseph Bailey; 22 (top) Bruce Dale; 22 (bottom) art by Ken Marschall. All other photographs courtesy of Bob Ballard.

BLAKEY: 25 and back cover Jeffrey John Fearing; 26 Saba Press Photos; 28 courtesy of Creative Communication; 29 Jeffrey Macmillan/*U.S. News & World Report*. All other photographs courtesy of Michael Blakey.

BOWLES: 30 Kenneth L. Bowles; 31 and back cover, 32, 33, and 34 Sea World staff; 35 (top) Scott A. Eckert. All other photographs courtesy of Ann Bowles.

DOUBILET: 37 and back cover Nicky Konstantino. Childhood photo and all other photographs courtesy of David Doubilet.

GOODALL: 44 Vanne Goodall; 45 John Giustina/The Wildlife Collection; 46 and 49 Hugo van Lawick; 47, 48, 50, and 51 Michael K. Nichols/NGP; back cover Ken Regan/Camera 5.

JOUBERTS: 52 (left) Eric Joubert; 52 (right) William Gibson; 53, 57, 58, 59, and back cover Jenny Song; 54 Dereck Joubert; 55 Denis van Eyssen; 56 Beverly Joubert.

NOVACEK: 62, 63, 64, 65, and 67 Louie Psihoyos. All other photographs courtesy of Michael Novacek.

REINHARD: 68 Walter Reinhard; 69 Jackie Shaffer; 70 Eduardo Pareja; 71 Ivan Vigouroux; 72 Constance Ayala; 73 José Antonio Chávez; 74 Louis Glauser; 75 and back cover José Antonio Chávez. All other photographs courtesy of Johan Reinhard.

WEST: 76 Constance West. All other photographs courtesy of Rick C. West.

ZARINS: 82 Marta Biegast; 85, 86–87, and back cover James Stanfield; 84 courtesy of JPL/NASA; 88 George Ollen/courtesy of Dr. Ronald G. Blom/JPL. All other photographs courtesy of Juris Zarins.